The Logic of English Prepositions Workbook

Exercises to Help you Feel the English Language

By J. Daniel Moore

The Logic of English Prepositions Workbook*: Exercises to Help you Feel the English Language*

Original Cover Design by Chongho Lee

Contact Information: contact@jdanielauthor.com

Table of Contents

This book is dedicated to my parents. I love you.

Introduction

This book is designed to be used with the book: *The Logic of English Prepositions: Intuitively Understand and Feel English like a Native Speaker*. This book contains many different exercises that you can use in order to help you master the logic of each preposition. However, this book is only one tool and you still have to practice using the prepositions and their logic in speaking and writing. There's a big difference between understanding something and being able to use it yourself.

Each exercise in this book has instructions and an answer section. The answers are fully explained, just like in the main book. The answer sections are directly after the exercises so that you can more easily check your answers without having to go to the back of the book. I recommend that before you do each exercise, get a piece of paper and a pen or open a blank word document so that you can write down your answers. If you check the answers and you made a mistake, try to understand why you made that mistake before reading the description. This will help you learn and remember better.

Like in the main book, I try to explain everything as clearly as possible, but because this book is based on the previous one, I assume that you already know a lot of the information. If you're using this book before finishing *The Logic of English Prepositions*, that's fine. That book is also a reference that you can use to find more information and check any details. You can finish that book and then use this one, or you can use this book and then search for more information in the main book when you need it. Just remember, the more time you spend thinking about the logic and practicing, the more familiar you'll become with these ideas, which will start to make things clearer, but it will take a little bit of time.

NOTE: When you're learning any skill, it's not about always getting the answer correct and trying to avoid every mistake. That's what schools teach us, and it's a horrible system, which is one reason why most people can't have a basic conversation after 4+ years of language classes. Relax, do your best, and if you make any mistakes, learn from them.

Confusing Prepositions 1

Instructions: Each section uses only two prepositions. You have to choose the correct one. Sometimes, both are right, but the meaning might change.

IN vs ON

1) You're in/on my chair.
2) Please explain the idea in/on your own words.
3) I live in/on the mountains.
4) What's in/on your mind?
5) What did you have in/on mind?

IN vs AT

1) He dies in/at the end of the movie.
2) It's in/at the middle.
3) I measured the length of the wall in/at inches.
4) In/At the future, you should be more careful.
5) I'm studying in/at that school.

TO vs AT

1) I'm good to start if you are. / I'm good at starting if you are.
2) He started dancing to/at the music.
3) He always looks to/at me for help.
4) The price could fall to/at $50.
5) There's a lot to/at learning a language that the average person doesn't know.

TO vs FOR

1) Take it to/for him.
2) To/For a cellphone from the 90's, it actually works really well.
3) (A soccer match:) The score is two to/for three.

4) I'll give you $20 <u>to do</u> it. / I'll give you $20 <u>for doing</u> it.
5) (End of the American Pledge of Allegiance:) "With liberty and justice <u>to/for</u> all."

ON vs ABOUT

1) There are a lot of interesting things to say <u>on/about</u> that topic.
2) There's just something <u>on/about</u> this math problem that I don't understand.
3) Think <u>on/about</u> it and tell me your answer tomorrow.
4) (During the news:) She's reporting <u>on/about</u> the new library.
5) He's walking <u>on/about</u> the grass.

Answers and Explanations

IN vs ON

1) You're **in** my chair. → Surprisingly, we use the preposition "in" here. This is something that confuses a lot of English learners. Of course, it's perfectly logical to think that we should use the preposition "on". You're physically sitting on top of a surface. However, the English language looks at chairs (and other kinds of seats) as personal containers. There are times when you can use the preposition "on", but the preposition "in" is more common. Remember, it can depend on the context and exactly what you want to say. But why do we use the preposition "in"? Think of an armchair (a chair that has spots on the side for your arms to rest on). You're inside the space that's created by the chair. When we think of a place that you sit as a "seat", that's a space that you occupy. This is true even if you sit on the grass. As long as you label a specific spot on the grass as a "seat", it becomes a space for sitting.

2) Please explain the idea **in** your own words. → Remember that languages are containers. We speak in English, in Spanish, etc… We don't always need the preposition "in", because it's not always needed (for example, "I speak English"; see group six in the main book for more information). When we say, "in your own words", it means that you heard or read something and then someone tells you to explain what you heard or read, but using your words, not the words that you heard or read. For example, you read a paragraph from a book and you have to explain what you read without saying exactly what the author said. Just like you can speak in English, you can put things in(to) your own words. Your words become the container that carry the message that you're trying to communicate.

3) I live **in** the mountains. → When we say "mountains" (plural), we usually use the preposition "in". The plural creates an area and you live somewhere in that area. This is because "mountains" is about a mountain range and not a particular mountain. However, if we use the word "mountain" (singular), we use the preposition "on", because it's like you're physically on top of the mountain. If you use the preposition "in" with the word "mountain", it means "inside the mountain", meaning under the ground or in a cave. In reality, you can say, "I live in the mountains" or "I live on the mountain" and they mean the same thing because they're so close.

4) What's **on** your mind? → This is a strange one and it's an idiom. Most of the time, your mind is an abstract container that's holds your thoughts. However, the phrase, "What's on your mind?" means that I want to talk to you about something that's important. If it's important, then it has some "weight". We even have a phrase: "Something's been weighing on my mind..." So in this context, whatever the important thing is that I want to talk about, it's "pressing downward" onto my mind, which causes stress.

5) What did you have **in** mind? → Now we can use the preposition "in" and not the preposition "on". This one is easier. Thoughts and ideas are in your mind, which is a container in this case. When we use this phrase, it means that someone has a plan and I want them to tell me what that plan is. For example: "I think I have a way that we can make a lot of money." "Really? What did you have in mind?"

IN vs AT

1) He dies **at** the end of the movie. → The end of something is a specific point.

10

2) It's **in** the middle. → We use the preposition "in" with the word "middle" because we're talking about the space or period of time that's half-way between two points, which is like the middle of a container. The two points (beginning and end, for example) are like the sides of the container, so we usually use the preposition "at" because they're specific points. The middle is also a specific point, but because it's between the other two, it's like it's "inside" the area of those two point.

3) I measured the length of the wall **in** inches. → Remember that the preposition "at" can be about a specific point of measurement. Here we're talking about the type of measurement ("inches" → "feet" → "yards"; "centimeters" → "meters" → "kilometers"; "Celsius" → "Fahrenheit"; etc…). Whichever type we use, all the specific measurements are inside that type. This is related to the "new environment/scale" idea that's in the explanation of the maps in Appendix B of the main book.

4) **In** the future, you should be more careful. → The future isn't a specific point in time. We can talk about a specific point in the future ("at 9:00 next Monday"), but the past, present, and future are containers that hold specific moments.

5) I'm studying **at** that school. → This is another one that confuses many English learners. Note that it is possible to use the preposition "in" with "school", but the context will be a little different and the logical relationship will be a little different. In this case, we use the preposition "at" because that specific school is the specific location that you go to learn/study. The purpose of this sentence is to talk about the location where you learn (this school not a different school).

TO vs AT

1) I'm good **to start** if you are. → This is short for "in order to". "I'm good" in this context means "I'm ready". This is the same idea as "about ready to start", but without the "about"/"scope" idea. So we have "to be ready" + "to" + "start", where the word "to" points to the action of starting and connects it to the idea of being ready.

2) He started dancing **to/at** the music. → The preposition "to" is more common in this case, but they both work in this context. If we use the preposition "to", it means that he's moving his body according to the rhythm of the music. If we use the preposition "at", it means "at the same time that the music starts **and** because the music starts". This is from group three in the main book.

3) He always looks **to** me for help. → Normally, we use the preposition "at" with the verb "to look". In this context, however, we use the preposition "to". "Look at me" means that I'm that target of his vision. But when we say, "Look to me", it means that he looks at what I do or asks me for advice so that he can make good decisions. So I'm the end point, but not the target. My actions are the target. In fact, we can change this sentence a little and use the preposition "at": "He always looks at what I do when trying to make a decision", for example.

4) The price could fall **to/at** $50. → Both of these can work in this sentence, but the meaning is different. "Fall to" means that the current price is higher than $50 and it might decrease to $50. "Fall at" means that the price is currently below $50, but it's increasing and when it reaches $50 (in other words, when it's at $50), it might start decreasing. $50 is the point (amount) at which the price starts decreasing.

5) There's a lot **to** learning a language that the average person doesn't know. → When we say that there's a lot to something, it means that there's a lot of information, truth, or something similar. In this case, we're saying that the average person thinks learning a language doesn't involve a lot. Sure, it might be hard, but maybe most people think that you can just learn grammar and then you'll become fluent, for example. There's a lot more to it than that, as you know. Also notice that we're using "to" + "-ing" because the preposition "to" and the verb aren't connected. This belongs to group seven in the main book. Also notice that we can say this sentence another way: "There's a lot to learn when learning a language…" In this case, we're saying that there's a lot to learn, meaning a lot that you have to learn. "A lot to learning" is a little different. It's not just about what you have to learn, but also about what you have to do (in order) to learn it (for example, textbooks, teachers, speaking practice, pronunciation practice, etc...).

TO vs FOR

1) Take it **to/for** him. → If we use the preposition "to", he's the end point (the receiver). If we use the preposition "for", you're taking it somewhere instead of him taking it somewhere (exchanging one basis for another basis).

2) **For** a cellphone from the 90's, it actually works really well. → The is the preposition "for" as a basis. Based on the fact that this phone was made in the 90's, you would expect that it wouldn't work well, but it does. In other words, it works well despite the fact that it was made in the 90's.

3) (A soccer match:) The score is two **to** three. → This is a comparison. One team has two points and the other team has three points. When you compare them, you start with the first team's score/points, which is two. From that score, you look at the second team's score, which is three points. From one team to the other team, the score is two to three.

4) I'll give you $20 **to do** it. / I'll give you $20 **for doing** it. →
If we use the preposition "to", it's short for "in order to". This
is an example in which "in order to" and the preposition "for"
both work.

5) (End of the American Pledge of Allegiance:) "With liberty
and justice **for/to** all." → This is the same as saying, "It's for
you". In the main book, we saw the sentence, "Did Tom leave
a box here for me?" Why do we have liberty and justice? To
protect people. Who are liberty and justice for? Everyone. The
purpose of having liberty and justice is to protect everyone, so
we say, "liberty and justice for all".

The preposition "to" can also work. I've always said
"for all", but some people, like my brother, say "to all". This
just shows once again how closely connected these two
prepositions are. Of course, if we use the preposition "to",
we're simply saying that "all" (meaning "everyone") is the end
point that receives the liberty and justice.

ON vs ABOUT

1) There are a lot of interesting things to say **on/about** that
topic. → Both of these work here, but the meaning changes.
You know that when we're talking about a topic, we can often
use both of these prepositions and the meaning doesn't change.
For example, "This is book is on/about Gandhi". However, in
this case, we're talking about saying something. The verb can
be very important and it can directly affect which preposition
we use and/or what each preposition means. This is because
the verb is usually a key part of the context. "To say something
on a topic" means that you're going to discuss the topic itself.
For example, if the topic is Gandhi, we can talk about his life,
his beliefs, etc… "To say something about a topic" means that
the scope is the topic instead of the topic being the scope. In
other words, instead of talking about Gandhi's life and all that,
you might say something like, "Gandhi's life was really

14

exciting", or "I don't care what Gandhi did". So, "on" in this context means that you're discussing things inside the topic, but "about" means that you're talking about the topic itself, meaning that the topic is the topic.

2) There's just something **about** this math problem that I don't understand. → The math problem is the scope. Inside that scope, there's something that you don't understand. For example, $2X = 6$. To find the answer, we divide $2X$ by 2, which means we have to divide 6 by 2 also, so $X = 3$. In this case, maybe the thing that you don't understand is why we divide by 2 on both sides. That's something that's inside the "scope" of the math problem.

3) Think **on/about** it and tell me your answer tomorrow. → Both of these can work here, but there's a small difference. "Think about" isn't a phrasal verb because "about" is simply the preposition that the verb "to think" usually uses. We already know why we use the preposition "about" in this case: the thing that you're thinking about is the scope of your thoughts and everything else that you could think about is outside of that scope. In other words, if you're thinking about trees, your not thinking about cars.

The phrasal verb "think on" is a little different. It means, "Think about it <u>and</u> make a decision about it". If you have to make a decision, there's some kind of abstract "weight" that you're putting on that thing. This is also similar to "work on". You're actively thinking about something and trying to make a decision. So you're not just thinking, you're processing what the best decision would be. The process of deciding is active.

4) (During the news:) She's reporting **on** the new library. → When we use "report" as a verb ("to report"), we use the preposition "on". When we use "report" as a noun ("a/the report"), we can use both the prepositions "about" and "on". As a noun, it's like a book: "This report is on/about Gandhi".

15

But when we use the verb "to report", we say that you're reporting "on" something. Why? Well, of course it's the active topic and it's also the focus, but that's also true when we use the word "report" as a noun. The preposition "about" should work perfectly fine, but we don't use it here. We say "to report on" because it's a chunk. For some reason it's a set chunk when "report" is a verb, but it's more flexible when "report" is a noun. Languages aren't perfect and sometimes things like this happen. The important thing is that the logic of the preposition "on" works perfectly.

5) He's walking **on/about** the grass. → Both of these work, but the meaning is different. "On the grass" means that the grass is the surface. We're not talking about where he's going, just that he's walking and the surface that he's walking on top of is the grass. "About the grass" means that he's on top of the grass, but also that he's walking around without a specific end point (destination). This is the same as saying "around the grass" with the meaning of "around the city" or "around the world". In those contexts, there might be a specific end point, but there are multiple specific end points, so we get the same basic idea of "from place to place". Of course, "around the grass" is more common, but the preposition "about" works.

Multiple Choice

Instructions: Every sentence in this exercise only has **one** possible answer. Some of the questions will be difficult, but remember, we don't just want to apply what seems generally logical. We want to apply how English uses the logic. As you answer each question, even if the answer is obvious to you, try to think how the logic of each answer might apply according to the personality of English.

1) <u>For / From / By / On / With</u> everyone's help, we raised enough money!

2) Are you alright? You seem a bit <u>under / off / out</u>. (It seems like something's a little wrong or unusual.)

3) When I got home, I was so tired that I passed <u>off / under / out / away / down</u>.

4) We're having a party <u>in / by / at / to / for</u> my house tonight.

5) He put paint all <u>over / on / in / around</u> my face.

6) Please turn <u>out / up / in / over / on / for</u> your homework.

7) I was <u>off / on / in / by / around</u> my bike when I crashed.

8) Here are some ways <u>for / by / with / to</u> learn a language.

9) I can't believe it! I think I need to sit <u>up / on / down / out / at</u>.

10) My birthday's <u>on / in / around / at</u> the 5th.

11) A pie baked <u>with / from / for / of</u> love.

17

12) You've been working too much. You should take some time <u>out / in / to / off / for</u>. (Take a short vacation)

13) That company is <u>in / over / by / under / with / on / of</u> new management.

14) Fold <u>out / around / up / in / on</u> your clothes and put them away.

15) She's <u>under / in / off / with / on / for</u> a diet.

Answers and Explanations

1) **With** everyone's help, we raised enough money!

WITH: The logic of the preposition "with" is "together". Remember that that's the most basic idea, but the logic can apply abstractly. In this case, let's say that I want to raise money for a charity that helps homeless people. "To raise money" means that you ask people for donations. So, imagine that I want to raise $1,000 so that I can donate that money to the charity. I ask other people if they will donate or if they will help in some other way, like asking other people to donate. If we reach the $1,000 goal, then we "raised enough money". But that was only possible with everyone's help. Their help is added to the effort of trying to raise $1,000. In other words, we're bringing their help and the goal together. Specifically, you can think of this as "using" everyone's help, but we don't say "using everyone's help", so it's an abstract connection.

FOR/FROM/BY/ON: The preposition "for" is about either a basis or a purpose. The idea of a purpose ("for the purpose of everyone's help") clearly doesn't work here, but you might think that the idea of a basis does work. In a way, it does, but we don't use the preposition "for" in this context. It's possible, but it sounds more like that older use of the preposition "for" that we mostly only use in poetry.

The preposition "from" is a good guess, but it doesn't work. Why? Remember that the logic of the preposition "from" is an "origin point" or a "start point". It makes sense to think that successfully reaching the goal came from everyone's help, and that's true. But in this sentence, we're not talking about the help as the origin/start point. We're talking about the help as something that we combine with the goal (in order) to successfully reach the goal. However, if we change the sentence and talk about it a little differently, the preposition "from" can work: "We were able to reach our goal with all of the help from our volunteers". But notice that we're still using the preposition "with". We only use the preposition "from" in

19

this sentence because we're saying "the help from our volunteers". We're specifying where the help came from.

As you know, the preposition "by" is very abstract. The closest group that can possibly apply here is group one ("an abstract medium that's a cause/source"). Unfortunately, it doesn't quite work here. It's logical, but we don't use it. Why? Because we're not looking at it as the help coming from everyone. That's true, but the focus is on using everyone's help (in order) to reach the goal.

Lastly, the preposition "on" just doesn't make any sense here.

2) Are you alright? You seem a bit **off**. (It seems like something's a little wrong or unusual.)

OFF: Remember that group three of the preposition "off" is "'away from' a center point/to the 'side' of a center point". That's what we're saying here. There's the normal way that someone behaves, but if they seem "off", it means that they're behaving in a way that's not normal. For example, maybe they're getting sick and that effects how they behave.

UNDER: The preposition "under" isn't a bad guess, but it's not correct. However, in a context like this, the prepositions "off" and "under" do share some space, just not exactly in the same way. For example, we have a phrase, "to feel under the weather", which means that you feel a little sick or you feel like you're not quite in good health. So, if you feel under the weather, it might make you seem a bit off, but these are two different ideas.

OUT: The preposition "out" by itself doesn't work. However, we can say, "You seem a bit out of it". This phrase means the same thing. It can work because if everything is normal, then you're behaving inside the container/limits of how you normally behave. But if you seem out of it, then it's like you're not in that container because your behavior is different than normal. In other words, it's like you left (went outside of) the normal container and entered the "not-normal"

20

container, so people notice that there's something different. Remember that when the preposition "out" isn't just an outward direction, it means that something is moving from inside one container to inside another container, which means that it's moving from outside the second container to outside the first container at the same time.

3) When I got home, I was so tired that I passed **out**.

      OUT: In this sentence, we use the preposition "out". The phrasal verb "pass out" means that you lose consciousness. However, in English, there are two different ways to pass out. The first is the same as the verb "to faint". This might happen when you're so surprised, scared, or exhausted, but you don't intend to lose consciousness. It just happens even if you don't want it to. The second way is when you (usually) intentionally go to sleep. In the sentence, "When I got home, I was so tired that I passed out", we're using "pass out" in the second way. I came home, went straight to bed, and fell asleep immediately.

      But why do we use the preposition "out"? I was conscious/aware. This idea is often connected to the preposition "on" (positive state/active state), but remember that the prepositions "on", "off", "up", "down", and "out" are very closely related and sometimes we get strange results. So, instead of saying "I passed off", we say, "I passed out". If you're conscious, then you're in a certain state of awareness, but when you're asleep, you're unaware. This is like a light. Conscious/aware = the light is on; unconscious/unaware = the light is off. But it makes sense. Remember that we can say "Turn the light off" or "Turn the light out". The preposition "off" is more common, at least in American English, but the idea is the same. We use the verb "to pass" because your consciousness passes from being in a state of awareness to unawareness. In other words, you left the container of "consciousness/awareness".

OFF: We just talked about the fact that we use the preposition "out" instead of "off" in this context. The logic of the preposition "off" works perfectly fine, but English doesn't apply it here. This is because 1) the logic of the preposition "out" can also work, and 2) we're using the verb "to pass". When we use phrasal verbs, it's not just about the preposition, it's also about the specific verb. They work together to create a new meaning. In fact, we also have the phrasal verb "to pass off", which means something completely different.

UNDER: We can use the preposition "under" with the verb "to pass", but not as a phrasal verb. This is just the basic use of "under". For example, if someone is sitting next to you at a table, you can pass (give) someone a piece of paper under the table so that no one else sees you do it.

However, remember that we have phrasal verbs like "bring up" (meaning "to mention"). The logic works in that case because it's like the idea was under the surface of your mind, or more simply that it wasn't the active topic of conversation, so the preposition "up" is connecting to the preposition "on". Because we have phrases like this, it is possible to apply the logic of the preposition "under", but we simply don't use it that way with the verb "to pass". If you remember from the main book, we do have phrasal verbs like "put under", meaning "to sedate", which is when you use drugs to make a person or an animal lose consciousness. So these ideas are definitely related, but they're used in different contexts.

AWAY: The phrasal verb "pass away" means "to die". One way that you can think about this is that it's like we're moving forward in time, but the person who passes away is "left behind".

DOWN: "Pass down" is a phrasal verb (we saw it in the main book), but it's not related to being conscious/aware.

4) We're having a party **at** my house tonight.

AT: We use the preposition "at" because we're talking about the specific location of the party. But remember that the preposition is about a specific point and/or a "bubble", which means the area that's inside of a specific point. So it doesn't matter if you have the party inside the house, outside the house in the front yard or outside the house in the back yard. In all of those cases, the location of the party is still your house, which includes the area around it. You can specify if the party is only in one of those areas: "inside" (not "in my house"), "in the front yard" or "in the backyard".

IN: See the previous explanation.

BY: This one can work because it's possible to have a party somewhere that's close to your house, but I don't think anyone would say, "We're having a party by my house tonight". Why? Because it's not specific. If you tell someone that, they know that the party will be somewhere near your house, but they won't know exactly where to go. However, you can say something like, "We're having a party at the park (that's) by my house tonight". Notice that we're still being specific and saying "at the park", but we're adding extra information: Which park? The one that's near my house.

TO: The preposition "to" is about an end point, which usually implies a direction. We're talking about the specific place where the party is located, which is just a specific point (and/or bubble). We know that the logic of the prepositions "to" and "at" are closely related, but in this case, we're not talking about the party as a destination. That would be a sentence like, "Are you going to the party tonight?"

FOR: We could apply the "purpose" part of the logic here, which would mean that we're having the party for the house, like I have a party for my birthday. Obviously, that doesn't really make sense here. You think that we can use this meaning when we move to a new house, for example, and so we want to celebrate and invite the neighbors so that we can meet them. But we have a special phrase for that: "house-warming party". For example, "We're having a house-warming party tonight". Notice that we don't need the preposition "at" because the location (the house) is implied.

5) He put paint all **over** my face.

OVER: Remember in the main book that we saw the example sentence, "Her face was covered with chocolate". One of the alternative sentences was, "There was chocolate all over her face." This is the same. This time, instead of chocolate, we're talking about paint and the paint covers the entire surface of my face or most of my face. There's paint from the top of my face to the bottom and from the left side to the right side.

ON: This one can work, but it's slang and doesn't exactly sound correct. Of course, the reason why it's possible is because my face is a surface.

IN: Obviously he's not putting the paint inside of my face.

AROUND: This one can also work, but not as well as the preposition "over". In this case, it sounds a little more like a circle around the edge of your face, but it can mean that your face is covered with paint. However, the preposition "over" is the most common and best preposition in this sentence.

6) Please turn **in** your homework.

IN: When we say, "Turn in your homework", it means that the teacher wants you to give them the completed homework that you did after the previous class. The homework is in your possession and you have to "turn" that possession to the teacher, meaning that now the teacher has it. You can also think of it a different way. Notice that we say that the teacher gives out the homework. You have to return the homework to the teacher in the next class. So, we say, "Turn in your homework". You're returning it to the teacher's possession, which is an abstract container in this context.

Note that in the main book I told you not to confuse the preposition "of" with the idea of "possession". This is another good reason for that because in this context, we're using the preposition "in" with the idea of "possession".

OUT: The phrasal verb "turn out" has a few different meanings, but none of them work here. In the previous

24

explanation, we saw that the teacher first gives out the homework, so it makes more sense to in this case to use the preposition "in" when you give the homework back to the teacher. Notice "give back" in this context is similar to "return" because the preposition "back" can mean "again, but in the opposite direction" and the "re-" part of a verb often means "again" (but not always!). Combine "re-" with the verb "to turn" and we have the idea of "give back", "go back", "come back", or even "throw (a ball) back".

UP: The preposition "up" is a good guess. You might think that we can use it because the preposition "up" can often mean "creation" or "completion". In this case, you completed the homework. But notice that we're not talking about completing the homework. We're talking about returning the already completed homework to the teacher. For example, maybe you only finished half of the homework. You can still turn that in so that you get some of the points.

OVER: The preposition "over" is very close, but we don't use it in this context. However, the phrasal verb "turn over" does exist and it has a very similar meaning. For example, someone drank too much at a bar and the bartender (the person who gives you drinks) say, "Turn over your keys. You're too drunk to drive". In contexts like these, it's more common to use the phrasal verb "hand over", but the idea is the same. Notice that when we use the preposition "over", we're not using the idea of "return". This is the biggest reason why we don't say, "Turn over your homework".

There is one possible way that we can use "turn over" with "homework", but only if we put the word "homework" between the verb and preposition: "Please turn your homework over". This means that the teacher wants you to physically turn the paper over. Let's say that instead of checking the homework themselves, they want to check it with the class. So the class start on the front of the page, but there's more on the back of the page. When it's time to look at the rest of the questions that are on the back, the teacher tells the class to turn the homework over, meaning "turn the page over to the other side".

ON: The preposition "on" doesn't make any sense here, unless your homework was to build a robot, for example.

FOR: The only way that this makes sense is if the teacher requires the students to turn their bodies (probably in a full circle) in order to receive the homework, which is possible, but extremely unlikely. The logic in that case would be the "purpose" part of the logic of the preposition "for".

7) I was **on** my bike when I crashed.

ON: You're physically on top of the bike when you ride it.

OFF: If you're off of your bike, then you can't crash.

IN: You can't be inside your bike.

BY: If you're by your bike, then you're off of it, so you can't crash. However, maybe you were on a skateboard and the place where you started to crash was near your bike. This is possible, but extremely unlikely, especially because there needs to be a very specific reason why you even mention your bike.

AROUND: This is exactly the same the previous explanation. Remember that the preposition "around" in a context like this is similar to the preposition "by", but it's a larger area.

8) Here are some ways **to** learn a language.

TO: Because we're saying "learn" and not "learning", the preposition "to" is the only possibility.

FOR: Let's compare "to learn" and "for learning" (remember that we need the "-ing" form). The preposition "to" makes the verb "learn" the end point. The idea here is "in order to". As you know, we usually omit the words "in order". In this case, however, it sounds strange if we add the words "in order". Normally it sounds fine, just unnecessary. There are some sentences like this. If you try to test it because you want to see if "in order to" is the idea, but it doesn't sound good, "in order to" might still be the basic idea. But it makes sense. The sentence is about ways that you can learn a language. The purpose of these ways/ideas is so that you can learn a language. So, the idea of "in order to" is there.

But why can't we say "for learning" in this case? Remember that the preposition "to" is normally just an end point. But when we use it with "in order", the end point becomes a purpose. When we do this, the preposition "to" steals the purpose part from the logic of the preposition "for". It's still possible sometimes for the preposition "for" as a purpose to work, but remember that "in order to" isn't just about a purpose, it's also about the ability to do that action. We talked about all of this in group six of the preposition "to".

BY: "By learning a language" is a perfectly grammatical phrase, but it doesn't work here. The full sentence would be, "Here are some ways by learning a language", which doesn't make any sense. "By learning a language" sounds more like a you're learning a language (in order) to do something else, which might be true, but that's not the focus of this sentence. This sentence is about ways to learn a language, not the reasons why you're learning it.

WITH: "With learning a language" is also perfectly grammatical, but like the preposition "by", it doesn't work here, either. The logic of the preposition "with" is "together". The context in which we might use this phrase is the same as using the preposition "in". For example: "In learning a language, you have to study a lot" or "With learning a language, you have to study a lot".

In a context like this, the preposition "in" is much more common, but the preposition "with" is used a little more often when we're comparing. For example: "With learning a language, studying is easy, but with learning math, studying is hard." This simply means that studying a language is easier than studying math. We can also use the preposition "in" here.

When we use the preposition "in" in this kind of context, we know that we're talking about a process, and that process is a container, usually the container of another action.

27

However, we can also apply the idea of "together" because we're putting the idea of "studying" with the idea of "learning a language". As I said, the preposition "in" is more common here, but it is possible to use the preposition "with". Going back to the original sentence, "Here are some ways with learning a language", remember that it doesn't work in that context.

9) I can't believe it! I think I need to sit **down**.

   DOWN: In this context, someone hears about something that is very shocking. Remember when we talked about passing out because someone is really surprised by something? This is why you sit down, in case you pass out because the news is so big or shocking. Of course, we use the preposition "down", because the person was standing up, so they are lowering their body onto some solid surface.

   UP: "Sit up" exists, but not in this context. We use it when someone is lying (usually in bed) and then they move their body so that they are sitting. This isn't related to the idea of being shocked.

   ON: The preposition "on" is a good guess, and you can use it if you specify the thing that you're going to sit on. For example, "I think I need to sit on a chair." This is because the preposition "on" is connecting the verb "sit" to the word "chair", which is a surface. However, when you're shocked about something and you feel that you need to sit somewhere because of it, it's much more common to just use the preposition "down". This is because in this context, it doesn't matter where you sit, you just need to move your body downward onto any solid surface (in order) to support your body.

   OUT: The phrasal verb "sit out" also exists. However, it's used in a different context. It might be possible to use it in the context of being shocked about something, but it seems very unlikely. "Sit out" generally means that you won't participate in something, especially a sports match. You don't have to literally "sit". The idea is that instead of being active

28

and engaged (positive state/active state), or being <u>in</u>volved <u>in</u> that activity/event, you'll be inactive and not involved (like you're "sitting"), so you're outside of that activity/event.

<u>AT</u>: "I think I need to sit at" doesn't make any sense and even if you add something after it, it doesn't work in this context ("I can't believe it").

10) My birthday's **on** the 5th.

ON: This is the same as "on Thursday". The only difference is that instead of talking about a day of the week, we're talking about a day of the month. If I say "My birthday is on Thursday, the 5th", I'm specifying the day of the week AND the day of the month at the same time. On the calendar, we see "Thursday" and we see "the fifth" at the same time. It's the same day in this case. Remember that we can look at the calendar as a surface, but the main idea here is that we're talking about the day as being active (positive state/active state).

<u>IN</u>: This preposition simply doesn't work here. Remember that we usually use the preposition "in" for larger periods of time that are like containers. So, you can say, "My birthday is in September on the 5th." However, it's much more common and easier to say, "My birthday's (on) September 5th". The preposition "on" becomes optional, probably because it's right before the word "September", which usually uses the preposition "in".

<u>AROUND</u>: You can use the preposition "around" when talking about a day of the week or a day of the month, but it doesn't work here. You're birthday is on a specific day. The preposition "around" means that you don't know the specific day. So, you can say, "<u>His</u> birthday is around the 5th," but you know when your own birthday is.

<u>AT</u>: This preposition simply doesn't work here. Remember that we usually use the preposition "at" for more specific points in time, like "at 12:00". So, you can say, "My birthday's at 12:00 on the 5th." In this case, you're actually talking about the time of the birthday party.

11) A pie baked **with** love.

WITH: This phrase is a little strange, but it's perfectly natural. I you do something with love, it means that you made it for someone that you really care about and you put extra effort into making sure that it's really good. For example, a grandmother might bake a pie with love for her grandchildren. "Love" in this case is like an extra ingredient, so it's the same as saying, "A pie baked with apples", for example. The idea here is both "using" and "having". You put love into the pie ("using") and then the pie has that love ("having").

FROM: We know that when we talk about what something is made of, we can usually use either the preposition "of" for the preposition "from". However, when we say, "A pie baked with love", we're not talking about the ingredients ("materials") of the pie. In other words, the pie isn't made of/from love. Instead, we're saying that someone made the pie for someone that they love, so when they made it, they made it very lovingly and maybe in a special way.

FOR: If you use the preposition "for", the meaning would be a "purpose". It's very unlikely that we wold use this preposition in this sentence, but it is possible in a very specific context. For example, there's a guy or a girl that you really like and you want to impress them, so you make a cake specifically so that they will like you, too.

OF: This explanation is the same as the previous one.

12) You've been working too much. You should take some time **off**.

OFF: When we talk about working, we often use the preposition "off". Remember that we <u>don't</u> usually use the opposite and say "I'm on work", but the logic is implied implied when you work because your work is active at that time. In the main book, we saw the sentence, "I get off (of work) at 5". We can apply this same idea here. If you've been working too much, then your work has been active a lot and you've been very busy, which means that you're using a lot of energy. This can cause problems because we all need a break at some point. When we say, "take some time off", it means that you're going to stop working temporarily. This is usually a short vacation.

OUT: The phrasal verb "take out" has a few different meanings. We use "take time out" in a different context than "take time off". For example, "If you want to become fluent in English, you have to take some time out everyday (in order) to study and practice." This works because what you're doing is removing a certain amount of time from your schedule so that you can improve your English. That time is reserved for English and nothing else, so it's "outside" of your available free time. Of course, you put the time into your schedule, but doing that removes the time from the time that you have available. When we talk about making sure that you reserve some time for it, you're taking it "out", meaning that you're doing that thing and it's not an open time spot in your schedule.

IN: "Take some time in" doesn't make any sense. That sounds like you're the container, or maybe you have some container, you're taking the time into yourself or that container. Things like schedules, which are related to time, can be containers, but taking time itself into something else doesn't work. One context where it can work is "take something into consideration", which means that you have to be aware of something when trying to make a decision. For example, if you want to learn a language, but you also want to learn how to play the guitar and you work two jobs, before you decide to start learning a language, you might want to take time into consideration. Here, the word "time" is short for "the time you have available". Just remember, "take some time in" doesn't really work, especially not when talking about work.

TO: "Take some time to" do what? You need to add something after the preposition "to" in this case. For example, "You've been working too much. You should take some time (in order) to relax". In this context, it's common to keep the

31

preposition "off": "You should take some time off to relax". That sounds very natural.

FOR: This is similar to using the preposition "to". We need something after it and it's very common to keep the preposition "off": "You should take some time (off) for yourself". The difference between the prepositions "to" and "for" in this context is what it is that your talking about. With the preposition "to", we're saying "in order to <u>do</u> something", but with the preposition "for", we're saying "for the purpose of something" (not "for the purpose of doing something"). So, take some time off for yourself means that you're going to take a short vacation so that you can focus on what you need (in order) to keep working (sleep, relaxation, time with friends and family, etc...).

13) That company is **under** new management.

UNDER: The logic of the preposition "under" is 1) "a downward force", usually with the idea of "restricting" and 2) "lower than or less than". When we're talking about management, both of these ideas work, but the first one is the clearest and strongest idea. The purpose of managers is to set rules and guide people who have a lower position than them so that everything runs smoothly in the business. In other words, the lower-level employees can't just do whatever they want. They have to dress a certain way, behave a certain way, etc... These are restrictions that come from the management, which is a higher position. So the management's restrictions/rules/policies a pushed downward onto the employees, which makes them behave in a certain way, dress in a certain way, etc...

IN: If anything, the management is inside the company, not the company being inside the management.

OVER: Of course, the preposition "over" doesn't work because it's the opposite of the preposition "under".

BY: The preposition "by" doesn't make any sense here.

WITH: The preposition "with" is a good guess. You might think that we can take "company" and "management" and put them together. It's definitely logical, but in this context, English doesn't like it. However, if we change the context a little bit, it can work. For example, "That company will do really well with the new management." We can also say, "That company will do really well under the new management". The reason that we can use the preposition "with" in this case is because we're not just talking about the company, we're talking about how well the company will do. More specifically, we're applying the idea of "to have" (group two in the main book). The company has new management and with that new management, it will do really well.

ON: The company isn't "on" the management (surface/platform). The idea of "positive state/active state" doesn't apply here, either.

OF: The company isn't part of the management and the management isn't the content of the company.

14) Fold (**up**) your clothes and put them away.

UP: The preposition "up" isn't necessary in this sentence, but it's one of those cases where we like to add it when we don't need it. It emphasizes the idea of "completion".

OUT: The preposition "out" doesn't work in this sentence. You might think that it means the opposite, but the opposite of "fold (up) is "unfold". The logic of the preposition "out" can apply, but English doesn't apply it here.

AROUND: This doesn't make any sense. Of course, you could wrap your clothes around something, like your arm, but it doesn't work in this sentence.

IN: The idea of a container doesn't apply here.

ON: We don't say "fold on your clothes". However, you can fold your clothes on something, like a table, which means that you put the clothes on a table (in order) to fold them. In that case, we're not saying "fold on", we're saying "fold" + "on the table".

15) She's **on** a diet.

ON: If you're on a diet, it means that you're eating certain foods and not others. You specifically choose what to eat for a special reason (usually to lose weight). So, it's like you're on a special platform that only has those foods. Any food that you're not allowed to eat is "off" that platform, so you can't reach them. Notice that if you decide to stop the diet, we say that you are now off of that diet. This is also a positive state/active state because the diet is like a light. Turn the diet "on" and it's active.

Also, remember that we have the phrase "off-limits", which means that you're not allowed to do something or have something. In fact, if you're on a diet, you can say, for example: "I'm on a diet, so cookies are off-limits".

UNDER: Ok, this is where things get really interesting. We know that the preposition "under" is a "downward force", often with the idea of "restricting". And that's exactly what a diet is: a set of restrictions about what you can eat. So, can we say, "She's under a diet"? No. The reason is because she's on an abstract platform called "diet". If I put my keys on a table, the keys aren't under the table, they're on top of the table.

However, what if we say this: "She's under strict dietary guidelines". This isn't the most common way to say it, but it works. Notice that we're not saying that she's under the diet, we're saying that she's under the guidelines. The guidelines restrict what she's able to eat. The word "dietary" is an adjective that simply describes what kind of guidelines we're talking about.

Also, the downward force of the preposition "under" pushes her onto the platform. Let's say that she really wants a cookie. Normally, she would just grab the cookie and eat it. But the downward force restricts her and causes her to stop and choose not to eat the cookie. Of course, she can eat the cookie anyway, but then she's not following her diet. She temporarily stepped off of the platform and ignored the restrictions. In English, we call this "cheating".

IN: It's perfectly logical to think of a diet as container, but the English language prefers to look at a diet as a platform and not a container.

OFF: This one can work, but without the article "a" in this sentence. We don't say, "She's off a diet" because if she was on a diet (any diet) it becomes specific. When she stops that diet, it's not "any diet", it's the specific diet that she was on. So, it's possible to say, "She's off (of) her diet".

WITH: This doesn't make any sense.

FOR: The preposition "for" can work if we use it as a basis with the meaning of "supporting" or "in favor of something". However, in this context, it's very uncommon. If you say, "She's for going on a diet", for example, it works a little better, but there are better and more common ways to talk about that. Instead of saying, "She's for going on a diet", it would be better to say something like, "She wants to go on a diet".

Choose All that Apply

Instructions: In the previous exercise, there was only one correct answer and you had to choose the correct one. This exercise is also multiple choice, but there are always at least two answers. This exercise will help you see how many prepositions can apply in a specific sentence. Sometimes the preposition will change the context and/or meaning and sometimes two or more prepositions are simply interchangeable with no change in meaning or context. Think about each preposition carefully and try to see if there's some way that it can work in the sentence, even if it changes the context. If there are any answers that work, but they're extremely unlikely in that specific context, don't pick those answers. I'll note these in the answers section.

1) My brother is going to pick her up at / in / on / by / around / over / from / about the store.

2) Her disease was brought up / on / about / down / in by poor diet.

3) I saw many interesting things when I was down / by / at / over / out / up in Panama.

4) We still have to check in / under / out / by / for / to / on / around / with the hotel.

5) I'm currently at / by / around / about / down / on / in / to the park.

6) She puts a lot of people off / up / down / around / under / over / in.

7) I met him by / at / off / down / on / around / in / over / of the beach.

8) Set all the books <u>on / in / by / at / around / from / over / under</u> the big box.

9) I simply can't put <u>up / down / off / on / in</u> that much money.

10) Keep <u>under / by / on / down / off / away from / at</u> the grass!

Answers and Explanations

1) My brother is going to pick her up **at / by / around / from** the store.

AT: This is the most basic answer. She's at the store, which is a specific physical location.

BY: If she's not at the store, but close to the store, or if my brother is going to pick her up at a place that is close to the store, then we can use the preposition "by".

AROUND: We can also use the preposition "around", which is just a larger area than "by". However, because the area is larger, the preposition "around" is less common in this context because if you're going to pick someone up, you need to know where they are.

FROM: If we use the preposition "from", then the store is the starting point or origin point. In this case, we're not looking at the store as just a specific location, but as a starting point. This is more common when you're not just picking someone up and then returning home with them. For example, you're going to leave your house, pick them up at the store, and then go to the beach. Either way, you can use the prepositions "at", "by", "around" and "from", but the preposition "from" is more common when you're going somewhere else (like the beach) after picking them up. This is because you're now going from the store to the beach instead of just going back home, so it's an extra point/location and you're leaving from that second point (in order) to go to the third point.

IN: Of course, you can pick things up in the store, like vegetables, but we don't use this for people. The reason is because you can't pick someone up (meaning drive to get them and take them somewhere else) from inside the store.

ON: This one can work if you have a helicopter and pick the person up from the roof of the store, but obviously that's something extremely rare, so we'll say that it doesn't work.

OVER/ABOUT: These two simply don't make any sense. However, you can use the preposition "over" with the prepositions "at", "by" and "around" (though "around" isn't common). For example, "My brother is going to pick him up over at the store". In this case, we're using the preposition "over" with the meaning of "over there".

2) Her disease was brought **on / about** by poor diet.

ON: The phrasal verb "bring on" has a couple of different meanings. In this context, it means the cause of something. So this is the same as saying, "Her disease was caused by poor diet". This is a little strange because the preposition "on" isn't usually about the cause of something, but this is a special case and it's still very logical.

The key is the verb "to bring". Remember, when we use phrasal verbs, it's not just about the logic of the preposition. It's also about the meaning of the verb and how that meaning combines with the logic (in order) to create a new or partially new meaning. So, we have the idea of the verb "to bring". That's the first part.

We know that the preposition "on" is always a positive state/active state. In this case, the disease is now "active" or "existing". We also know that the preposition "up" often connects to the preposition "on" and we can see how the idea of "creation" is close to the idea of a "cause". However, because we have the verb "to bring", we don't need to use the preposition "up" if we want to talk about the creation/cause of the disease. Instead, we can simply use the preposition "on" to talk about the disease being active/existing. So, the meaning that comes from the verb "to bring" replaces the meaning of the logic of the preposition "up" in this case.

Of course, the phrasal verb "bring up" also exists, but when we specifically use the preposition "up", the meaning changes and we use this combination in a completely different context. When we use "bring up", which means "to mention", we're making a topic active, so we need the preposition "up" (in order) to connect to the preposition "on" and now we're on that new topic that someone brought up (mentioned). It's like the verb "to bring" uses the preposition "up" (in order) to reach the preposition "on". But when we say "bring on", the verb "to bring" is enough and we can simply talk about the disease being active.

But why? The combination "bring up" has it's own meanings and contexts, so we can use another combination with "bring on" and use this new combination with new meanings and different contexts. We know that the prepositions "up" and "on" are very closely related and that can make things confusing sometimes. It's not about needing the preposition "up" (in order) to connect to the preposition "on". It's about using the specific logic of each preposition in different ways.

ABOUT: The phrasal verb "bring about" means "to cause something to happen". So it means the same thing as "bring on", except "bring on" has more uses. The question is: how does the verb "to bring" work with the logic of the preposition "about" (in order) to create the meaning of causing something to happen?

We know that the preposition "about" is a "scope". The key here is that this is one of the uses of the preposition "about" that's similar to the preposition "around" when we're talking about physical locations. There's a note in group two in the main book that talks about using "about" for approximate location. The preposition "around" is more common in that context. For example, "He lives somewhere around here", but not "about here". Also remember that we have sentences like, "All of his clothes were lying about/around the room". The version that uses "around" is more common in American English, but we can say it either way. In that sentence, the room is the scope.

Ok, what how does all of this connect to the phrasal verb "bring about"? She has a poor diet. That caused/created her disease. The diet already existed, but the disease didn't. Over time, her poor diet brought the disease into existence. More specifically, it brought the disease into her body. Her body is the scope, but the core idea here is that the disease now exists inside her body, so we can also say that the scope is existence, but limited to her body.

UP: We already talked about the fact that "bring up" is used in a different context. With the idea of "creation", which is similar to the idea of a "cause", the logic can definitely work, but English applies the logic to a different context because we have "bring on" in this context.

DOWN: "Bring down" means "to destroy" or "to defeat", depending on the specific context. Obviously it doesn't work in this context, because if her poor diet brings down her disease, then her poor diet destroyed the disease, and that's the opposite of what we're saying.

IN: This doesn't make any sense. You can say "Her disease was <u>brought into existence</u> by poor diet" (which we don't say, but it's grammatically correct), but you can't use just "brought in". We saw how her body or existence can be the scope, but remember that if we say that existence is the scope, the focus is limited to her body. There are probably other people who have that disease, so it already generally exists, but it didn't exist in her body before. So in this context we don't use the preposition "in" (in order) to talk about the disease coming into existence, at least not with the verb "to bring".

3) I saw many interesting things when I was **down / over / out / up** in Panama.

DOWN: We saw a sentence like this in the main book (preposition "down", group one). Remember that we can talk about a location being "up" or "down" compared to where you are right now. If I'm in the United States, it's very natural for me to say "down in Panama" because Panama is south of the US.

UP: This is the opposite of the previous explanation. If I'm in Brazil right now, I can say, "up in Panama".

OVER: This is the same as "up" and "down", but now we're talking about a location that is to the east or west of your current location. We often use this for very long distances. For example, if I'm in California, I can say "over in New York". If we're talking about Panama, maybe I'm in Africa, for example. However, it doesn't have to be exactly east or west. For example, in the southern/southwestern US, I can say "When I was over in Spain". I can also say, "When I was up in Spain". These both work because Spain is to the north of where I am, but it's also a long way to the east. So, the preposition "over" is about the directions east and west, and the prepositions "up" and "down" are about north and south.

OUT: This one is very interesting. If we say, "out in Panama", it sounds like you're talking about Panama as outside of something that you're normally in. In this case, it would be your home country. It makes sense: if you're from the United States but you're talking about being in Panama, Panama is outside of the United States. Another example to make this clearer: "My grandma grew up out in the countryside". You grew up in the city, which we know is like a big container. The countryside can also be an abstract container because it's a large area that you can be inside of.

Notice that we have three prepositions together in this sentence. This is something that doesn't happen all the time, but it's possible. The reason it's possible is because of the three types of uses of prepositions that you can find in the "How to Use this Book" section of the main book (regular preposition, false phrasal verb, and true phrasal verb). So, we have "grow up" (true phrasal verb) + "out" (regular preposition) + "in the countryside" (regular preposition). The preposition "in" is part of the rest of the sentence.

The preposition "out" in this case simply emphasizes or contrasts the fact that you're thinking from the perspective of living in a city. In other words, you're grandma grew up "out there", meaning outside of the city. But where outside of the city? In the countryside. So we see the prepositions "out" and "in" next to each other, but they have two completely different functions in the sentence.

Note that the preposition "out" doesn't have a specific direction. The only direction it has is an outward direction that

43

goes away from the inside of something (like a box, a city, or a country). So, the exact details of the context are important, but the basic idea is that the preposition "out" can replace the prepositions "up", "down", and "over" in a context like this.

BY: "By in Panama"? That doesn't make any sense. Notice, however, that you can replace the preposition "in" with the preposition "by": I saw many interesting things when I was down/up/over/out by Panama". If you say that, then you weren't in Panama, you were just close to Panama.

AT: The preposition "at" doesn't work at all. You can't even replace the preposition "in", because we need the preposition "in" (in order) to talk about being inside the country. The preposition "at" would be used for very specific locations inside the country, like a particular store, house, or other location (at the zoo, at the beach, etc...).

4) We still have to check **in / out / by / on / around / with / at** the hotel.

IN: Let's talk about the difference between the prepositions "in" and "into". We know that English speakers usually reduce the preposition "into" to the preposition "in" because the context is usually clear. For example, if a dog jumps into a lake, we can simply say, "The dog jumped in the lake." However, if a dog jumps into a puddle (a small pool of water that's on the ground), that means something different than if a dog jumps in a puddle. If you're in a lake, you can't jump when you're inside of it, so we can use the preposition "in" instead of "into". But a puddle is something that you can jump into and then once you're in the puddle, you can jump inside of it.

Another important point here: remember the sentence that we saw earlier, "Her disease was brought on by poor diet". We talked about why we don't use the phrasal verb "bring up" in that context. One of the reasons is because if we use the preposition "on" and "up" in different contexts, we can create different meanings even though they're so close. So, instead of using the preposition "up" (in order) to connect to the logic of the preposition "on", we can use the preposition "on" directly in a different context. The point here is that we can create more phrasal verbs if we use variations that we normally don't use, like using the preposition "into" instead of just the preposition "in".

Ok, now that we've talked about all that, let's talk about "check in" and "check into". We'll start with "check into" because that one is more common in the context of hotels. When we talk about checking into a hotel, it means that you go into the hotel, give the staff your information, get your room key, and go to your room. You're going to temporarily "live" in the hotel for some amount of time, which simply means that you'll be staying there. This can be for a night or longer.

Remember that the preposition "into" is a compound preposition ("in" + "to"), so we're using the logic of both prepositions together. The preposition "in" is about a container and the preposition "to" is about an end point. Think of the hotel as a box. You can put a book into a box. (We often say, "Put the book in the box" because in this context, especially with the verb "to put", the only possible meaning is "into", so it's clear that we mean "into" and not "in". We won't worry about that right now. The point is that we want to talk about the logic of "into", even if we only say "in".) So, the box is a container ("in") and the inside of that container is the end point/destination ("to").

When you check into a hotel, it's like you're temporarily putting yourself into a box. Of course, you can go outside, but you're officially "checked into" the hotel, so you're still in the abstract box. Unlike a book that's in(side) of a box, we're not talking about only being inside a physical container, but the basic idea is the same. We'll talk about leaving a hotel when we look at the preposition "out".

So if "check in" means officially getting a room and staying temporarily, what does "check in" mean? This is a little complicated, because depending on the context, "check in" can be short for "check into". For example, you check in at the airport, but you don't check into the airport because you're not staying there. Also notice that we only need the "to" part of the preposition "into" when you specifically say "the hotel" → "check into the hotel". But let's say that you and your friend are going to stay at a hotel for two nights and you're getting two different rooms. Your friend arrives at the hotel first and you arrive an hour later. Your friend sees you outside and asks, "Have you checked in yet?" Here, the context of the hotel is very clear and your friend isn't specifically mentioning the hotel, so we can reduce the phrasal verb "check into" to simply "check in".

But "check in" also has a different meaning. If you say, "check in the hotel", this isn't a phrasal verb. It's "check" + "in the hotel". It means that you're looking for something and you're going to look <u>inside</u> the hotel to see if it's there or not. Remember that both the prepositions "into" and "inside" can reduce to the preposition "in" if the context is clear. One of the meanings of the verb "to check" is "to make sure" and in this specific context you're making sure that something isn't inside the hotel by looking for it. So in this context, you can also say, "We still have to look in(side) the hotel", but with the specific purpose of making sure that the thing that you're looking for isn't there.

So, we can see that both "check in the hotel" and "check into the hotel" are possible, which means that both of them are correct answers in this exercise.

OUT: Similarly to "check in" and "check into", we also have "check out" and "check out of" in this context. Let's start with "check out of", because that one is more common when talking about hotels. When we say "check out of the hotel", it means the opposite of "check into the hotel". Notice that if we talk about the book in the box that we talked about earlier, it's the same: "Take the book out of the box". Remember, when you check into the hotel, it's like you're officially putting yourself into a box temporarily, so when you return the room key and leave the hotel, you're officially getting out of the box.

We know that we can often omit the preposition "of" and just use the preposition "out", but not always. In the case of the book in the box, we have to use the preposition "of". The exact details of when you can and can't omit the preposition "of" are complicated, but it's something that you can get used to if you pay attention to how people speak.

But what does the phrasal verb "check out" mean? If you check out a hotel, it means that you're going to look at it, probably go inside it, and see what the hotel has. Or it can mean that you go online (in order) to find more information about it, which includes looking at reviews that people have left. We saw a sentence in the main book: "Check out that guy in the pink shirt!" When you check out a hotel, the context is a little different, so the exact meaning is a little different, but these two sentences are very similar and the basic idea is the same.

Interestingly, because "check out" means that you're going to look at/inside the hotel, you can use it in almost the same way as "check in the hotel". For example, you're trying to find someone and you think they might be in the hotel, so you say, "Let's check out the hotel and see if he/she is in there". It feels a little different, but the meaning in this context is the same. But note that when we say "check out the hotel", "check out" is a phrasal verb, but when we say "check in the hotel", it's "check" + "in the hotel". This doesn't matter for the logic because the logic works either way, but it helps to know how things are used so that you can understand the meaning better.

BY: "Check by the hotel" is similar to "check out the hotel" and "check in the hotel". You're looking for something and you're going to look next to or around the hotel (in order) to see if it's there.

ON: You might think that "check on the hotel" is the same as "check by the hotel", but physically on top of it. That would be true, but in this context, "check on" is a phrasal verb with a different meaning. "Check on" can mean "on top of" (for example, "check on the table", meaning "look at the table (in order) to see what's on it"), but it doesn't work in this context. If you want to say "on top of" in this case, you have to say that specifically: "We still have to check on top of the hotel". This works similarly to "on the bus". Because "on the bus" usually means that you're riding inside the bus, you have to specifically say "on top of the bus" if you want to express that idea, unless the context is extremely clear (for example, you point to a man who's on top of a bus and say, "Look! There's a man on that bus!"

Ok, so what does "check on the hotel" mean? Let's say that you want to stay at a particular hotel when you visit France. However, this hotel is very busy and it's hard to reserve a room. So you decide to check online (in order) to see if there are any open rooms and there aren't; you check again the next day and there still aren't any; etc... When you go online (in order) to check, you're checking on the hotel, which is actually short for "check on the availability of open rooms in the hotel". A more common context that we use the phrasal verb "check on" in is with your children. Say your children went to bed an hour ago and before you go to bed, you want to make sure that they're ok. So you look into their room(s). This means that you're checking on them. Or maybe you're cooking and you want to make sure that the food isn't burning, for example, so you check on the food.

But why do we use the preposition "on" in these cases? The verb "to check" in these sentences means "to verify" or "to make sure". This means that you're looking at the status (state) of something. With cooking, this is if the food is done or not (or if it's burning); with children, it's about they're safety and what they're currently doing; with a hotel, it's the availability of a room.

We know that the preposition "on" is about a positive state/active state (in a neutral way, not a "good" way). We saw a sentence in the main book: "I'm working on a new book". "To work on something" means that you're focusing on that thing. So the book becomes an abstract platform that your attention is focused on. You're also <u>active</u>ly engaged in

48

creating the book. When we use the verb "to check", the context and the basic meaning are different, but the logic of the preposition "on" in this case is the same as in the phrasal verb "work on". This is because when you check on something, it's the current focus of your attention (on) and you're just quickly making sure that everything is ok (check).

AROUND: "Check around the hotel" is the same as "check by the hotel" and "check in the hotel". In fact, not only is it the same type of context, but it can mean both of those. "Around the hotel" in this case can mean "by the hotel", but a larger area. However, it can also mean that you're looking around inside the hotel, meaning that you're looking in different places that are inside the hotel.

What's the difference between "around the hotel" and "in the hotel" in this case? "In the hotel" sounds like you're just going to look anywhere in the hotel, or maybe you're going to look in a couple of different places that are inside the hotel. "Around the hotel" sounds like you're going to look everywhere in the hotel, or in many different places that are inside the hotel. This is similar to the idea of traveling around the world or driving around a city. However, we often use the prepositions "in" and "around" interchangeably in this context.

WITH: Let's say that you're traveling with your dog. Not all hotels accept animals. So, you call the hotel (in order) to check with them, meaning that you want to make sure that having a pet is ok. The preposition "with" means "together". You're bringing your question to them so that you can check (make sure) that it's ok to bring your dog.

UNDER: This is possible if you mean "in the basement", but that's not very common. It's more common to say "in the basement".

FOR: This is also possible if you're checking something for the hotel, meaning that you work there and you're checking on something or trying to find information about something that the hotel needs. For example, they want to know how much it would cost to build a pool, so you call someone who builds pools. You do this on behalf of the hotel.

However, note that not only is this uncommon when talking about hotels, but you also you usually need something between the words "check" and "for". For example, "I'm checking the price of pools for the hotel". Because of these reasons, this is not an acceptable answer for this exercise, but it is possible.

TO: The preposition "to" doesn't make any sense here.

5) I'm currently **at / by / around / in** the park.

AT: This is the most basic answer. Your specific location is the park. We can use the preposition "at" instead of the preposition "in" here because it's similar to a store: if you're in the store of directly outside of the store, you're still "at the store". It's like there's a "bubble" around the store because it's one location. We look at the park as one big location.

BY: You can also be by the park, which is like "next to".

AROUND: "Around the park" is like "by the park", but a larger area. Notice that the verb is very important. If we use the verb "to be", the meaning of the preposition "around" is similar to the meaning of the preposition "by". However, if we use the verb "to look" or "to search", for example, it can mean "look/search inside the park (in order) to find something".

IN: We don't usually say "I'm in the park". When we talk about stores, "I'm in the store" is useful information because you can go inside the building. But when we talk about parks, "in the park" isn't always useful. It depends on the verb. Instead of saying, "I'm in the park", we simply say, "I'm at the park". This is partially because a park is an open area and not a building and partially because I'm not talking about what I'm doing, I'm talking about where I am (my physical location = specific point/bubble, which includes "location").

But if you use the verb "to walk", for example, we usually say, "I walk in the park" instead of "I walk at the park". This is because you're walking inside the area of the park, and meaning that you're doing something inside of the park, so the

50

preposition "in" carries more useful information than the preposition "at" (more on this topic in question 7). But again, it all depends on the specific details of the context. Just don't forget that the verb can be very important even if it's not a phrasal verb.

However, there is one exception. Places like sports stadiums or theme parks (for example, Disneyland), are also parks. In that context, we can use "in the park" like "in the store" and "at the park" like "at the store".

ABOUT: Remember that when we're talking about physical areas, the prepositions "about" and "around" with the meaning "approximately" aren't usually interchangeable, so in this case, the preposition "about" doesn't work.

DOWN: It's possible to say, "I'm down at the park", or "I'm down by the park", but not "I'm down the park".

ON: We look at a park as a location and/or area. Yes, there's a surface (the ground), but English doesn't care about that. If you say, "I'm on the park", it sounds like the park has a roof.

TO: You can say, "I'm going to the park" or "I'm closer to the park (than something else)", but not "I'm to the park".

6) She puts a lot of people **off / down**.

OFF: The phrasal verb "put off" has a couple different meanings, but in this context is means that she does and/or says things that make people not like her. For example, she might be a really loud person or a really arrogant and judgmental person. The normal verb that we can use instead is "to repel".

But why do we use the preposition "off"? If your behavior repels someone, that person doesn't want to interact/engage with you. Remember that we often use the preposition "on" when talking about a topic, which is like an abstract platform, but it's also the current focus of the conversation. If no one talks to you, then they don't get into conversations with you, so there are no topics to be on. So, she

51

puts (places) people off of wanting to talk about any topics with her. They don't get on the platform at all and no topics become active. Another way to look at this that might be easier is that normally, people want to talk to you. But if you put people off, it means that the desire to talk to you is inactive, like a light that's turned off.

Lastly, remember that we have the idea of the "central platform". This idea is most strongly tied to the preposition "down" (group five), but it's also part of the prepositions "up", "on", and "off". For example, if you put people off, you can look at it as pushing people away from the central platform, which is where you are. See group five of the preposition "down" to review or find more information about this idea.

DOWN: The phrasal verb "put down" means that you say rude and hurtful things to people when they do or say something. The goal is usually to make the other person feel bad so that you can feel better about yourself, which is obviously not a very good or useful thing to do, but some people do it anyway. For example, your friend asks you if you want to go to the movies tonight. You say, "Duh. Why wouldn't I? It's Friday night. Don't ask stupid questions."

We know that part of the logic of the preposition "down" is a "downward/southward direction" or a "downward position". Both of these ideas can work here. What often happens when you put someone down is that you make them feel stupid, which can also negatively affect their self-confidence. So you're changing how they feel from a positive state to a negative state. We know that the positive state/negative state idea is not about "good"/"bad", but it can be in rare cases. So putting someone down can use the first idea (downward direction), because we're talking about the change, or it can use the second idea (downward position), because we're talking about the result after the change. You can also think of it as the connection between an active and inactive state. Their self-confidence was active enough to say, ask, or do something, but when you put them down, you're trying to make their self-confidence inactive.

52

UP: "Put someone up" does exist, but it doesn't work in this context, or at least it's extremely unlikely.

AROUND: This doesn't make any sense here. If there's more information, it might be able to work.

UNDER: This doesn't make any sense here. If there's more information, it might be able to work.

OVER: This doesn't make any sense here. If there's more information, it might be able to work.

IN: This doesn't make any sense here. If there's more information, it might be able to work.

7) I met him **by / at / on / around** the beach.

BY: "By the beach" is like "at the beach", but it's more similar to the meaning of "next to". Because we usually talk about the beach as a large area and not just the sand, the exact position of "by" and "at" aren't clearly separated. For example, "the beach" can include the ocean, the sand, the pier, a grassy area in front of the beach itself and any store that are across the street. If you're at least one block from the beach, you can say that you're by the beach.

AT: This is the most preposition here. Again, it includes all the things that are in the previous example, such as the pier and stores. Because the beach is usually more of an area than a specific point, the logic that applies is the idea of a "bubble". However, notice that if you look at that area from above, such as in a plane or from a satellite, the "bubble" is like a big, specific point.

ON: "On the beach" simply means "on top of the sand". In this case, we're talking about the physical beach itself and not the general area that we usually call "the beach". Remember that the prepositions help you say exactly what you want to say because they show the relationships between things. In this case, the relationship is between you and the physical sand of the beach, but if you use the preposition "at", for example, then the relationship is you and the area of the beach, not just the sand. Of course, just like you can say, "I'm at the store" when you're inside the store because that's still your location either way, if you're on the beach, you can also say that you're at the beach.

But notice that if you're talking on the phone and your friend asks, "Where are you?", if you say, "I'm at the beach", the don't know if you're on the sand, but if you say, "I'm on the beach", they know that you're actually on the sand and not on the pier, for example. Again, this is just like when you're at the store. "I'm at the store" isn't clear. Are you inside or outside? But "I'm in the store" tells the other person that you're specifically inside the store.

This is a good time to remember that the prepositions "at", "on", and "in" are very closely related and are tied together in many ways, but it depends on the specific context. Usually, the preposition "at" is a specific point, such as a location, but if you go into that location (like a store or some other building), then the preposition "in" is actually more specific than the preposition "at". But when we change the context, like talking about the beach, the preposition "on" becomes more specific than the preposition "at" (going downward on the cone of existence map that's at the end of the main book). One context is a building, so we use "in", because a building is a container. The other context is the physical sand of a beach, so we use "on", because the sand is a surface. If you haven't read the explanations of the map at the end of the main book, you might want to do that now. It shows how the smallest scale can become the largest scale, and this is another example of that. If this is confusing right now, don't worry about it. You'll start to see what I'm talking about as you continue to practice the prepositions and become more familiar with the logic and how they work throughout the whole language, but the map that's in the main book can help a lot, too.

AROUND: If you say, "I met him around the beach", it sounds like you're not really sure where you met him, but the closest place that you can think of is the beach. Of course, the preposition "around" in this case is like the preposition "by", but a larger area.

OFF: Of course, it's possible to use "off (of) the beach", but not in this context. The verb is "to meet", and we don't normally say, "I met him off the beach." If you're not on the sand, but you're at or by the beach, then that's what we say: "at the beach" or "by the beach", so the preposition "off" doesn't really give us any useful information. However, you can say, "I walked off (of) the beach", meaning that you were on the beach and then you walked until you weren't on top of the sand anymore.

DOWN: This one is possible, but very unlikely. It's possible because it's the same as saying, "I met him down the street", where "down" means "away from the central platform" (likely my house, or wherever I was before I went to meet with him, or even where I am now). In other words, you were both on the beach, but you had to go farther along the beach to meet him.

Of course, you could also say, "down at the beach", in which case "down" is not about a point along the beach. Instead, I met him at the beach, and the area/location that we call "the beach" is away from the central platform.

IN: "In the beach" means "inside the sand", so this one doesn't work here.

OVER: This doesn't really make any sense, because there would have to be something above the beach. However, just like with the preposition "down", you can say, "I met him over at the beach". This works exactly like the preposition "over" in the sentence, "My brother is going to pick her up over at the store".

OF: This doesn't make any sense.

8) Set all the books **on / in / by / around / over / under** the big box.

ON: The verb "to set" in this context means "to put" or "to place". If you set the books on the box, it means that you put the books on top of the box.

IN: This is short for "into". You're putting the books into the box.

BY: In this case, "by" and "next to" are almost the same thing because we're talking about a very small area. So you can think of this as "Put the books next to the box".

AROUND: It's possible that this can mean "by", but a larger area. However, we're talking about a small area, so making the area bigger doesn't make much sense. If you want to use that meaning here, you have to add a word like "somewhere": "Set all the books somewhere around the big box". When we say, "Set the books around the box", the preposition "around" means "surrounding" or "partially surrounding", which is the circle/semi-circle part of the logic, so it still works, but with a different meaning.

OVER: The preposition "over" works here, but it doesn't mean "on top of". That's the meaning of the preposition "on" in this context. The way that the preposition "over" works is if you have a shelf that's above the box, for example. "over the box" means "on the shelf that's over the box". The preposition "above" works exactly the same here.

UNDER: The preposition "under" also works, but in two ways. 1) You put the box on top of the books, so the books are now under the box. 2) Let's say that the box is on a shelf. "Under the box" in this case means "under the shelf that the box is on". The preposition "below" is the same, but only for meaning number two because this is the opposite of "above the box".

AT: You might be surprised, but the preposition "at" doesn't work here. Why? 1) Because it doesn't tell us anything useful, and 2) because the books can't be in the same specific location as the box. "In the box" is close, but the books can't be in the space that the physical sides of the box occupy. At this small scale, we usually need to use other prepositions because prepositions are about the relationship between things. So, "in" means inside or into the box, depending on the exact context and verb; "on" means on top of; "under" means below or that the box is on top of the books; etc... All of those possibilities tell us the exact relationship between the books and the box, but the preposition "at" is meaningless here.

FROM: It's possible to use the preposition "from", but not in this context and not with this verb ("to set"). If you want to talk about the books being in the box and then moving them somewhere else, you have to change the verb. For example, "Take the books from the box", which is usually followed by more information: "Take the books from the box and put them on the table". "From the box" in this case means "from the inside of the box to the outside of the box". Remember that the preposition "from" is about an origin point/start point, so "set the books from the box" doesn't work well because the idea of the verb "to set" (or "put"/"place") in this context means that you're moving the books to another location.

9) I simply can't put **up / down / in** that much money.
   UP: The phrasal verb "put up" has a lot of meanings. In this context, it means "to pay for something", usually for a special purpose. For example, a thief stole a painting and wants a ransom (money in exchange for the painting). The person who pays the ransom (in order) to get the painting back "puts up" the money.

What's the logic of the preposition "up" here? You need to pay for something (in order) to get something else back, so we can apply to idea of "completion". You're completing that transaction. The thing is yours, but someone took it, and now you're getting it back, so the process/transaction is complete.

   DOWN: In the main book, we saw the sentence, "I put $300 down on a new car" (group four). This is the same meaning of the preposition "down".

   IN: When we talk about putting in money, it means that you're contributing to a large payment. For example, you and your friends want to buy something special for one particular friend because it's their birthday. You want to buy something very expensive that costs $800. So you and all of your other friends contribute a part of the $800, which means that there's an abstract main container that you all put your money into. When we say, "I simply can't put in that much money", it means that whatever amount you're supposed to contribute is too much because you don't have that much money to spend. It's more common to use the phrasal verb "chip in", but "put in" also works.

OFF: The phrasal verb "put off" exists, as we saw earlier, but it doesn't work in this context.

ON: If you say, "put on that much money", it sounds similar to "put on weight" (gain weight) or "put on clothes". Remember that we have option to use the preposition "down", which connects to the preposition "on" in this context, so we don't actually need the preposition "on" and we don't use it here.

10) Keep **by / on / off / away from** the grass!

BY: In this case, the preposition "by" means "next to" or "near". Again, like with the books in question eight, we're talking about a small area. You might use this sentence if you're a parent and you're walking with your kids. Let's say that you want them to stay away from the street as you all walk, so you tell them to keep by the grass.

ON: Of course, grass is a surface, so you can be on top of it. Normally, people want you to keep off (of) the grass, but the preposition "on" can definitely work. Again, imagine that you're a parent. You don't want your kids to walk away and disappear when you're not looking, so you tell them to keep on the grass. This means that the edge of the grass becomes a barrier that they're not supposed to cross, but the focus of this sentence is to remain on top of the grass itself.

OFF: This is the most common preposition in this case. People take care of their lawns (the grass that's in the front and back of the house) and most people don't want you to walk on it so that it stays pretty.

UNDER: This one doesn't make much sense because you can't be under grass. There's probably some strange context where it's possible, but most of the time this just isn't possible.

<u>DOWN</u>: The only way this can make sense is if the grass is really tall and you have to hold it down for some reason. This is extremely unlikely, not just because of the context, but because of the fact that grass will usually stay down by itself after you push it down.

<u>AWAY FROM</u>: The preposition "from" can work, but only if we add the preposition "away". This is because of the verb "to keep". You're already off of the grass <u>and</u> away from the grass, meaning that you're not near it. However, "keep away from the grass" isn't common because most of the time, people want you to stay off of the grass, but there's no problem if you're just by the grass.

<u>AT</u>: Like we saw with the books and the box in question eight, the preposition "at" doesn't tell us anything. In a very special context, it's possible, but most of the time it simply doesn't work. This is because if you say "at the grass", where are you? On the grass? By the grass? If you're on the grass, where on the grass are you?

Fill-in-the-Blanks

Instructions: Fill in the blank spaces with the correct preposition(s). There's often <u>more than one</u> correct answer. Sometimes, a preposition is possible, but extremely unlikely in that specific context. Ignore those.

1) Here are some techniques ___ learning a language faster.

2) The dog hid ___ the table.

3) I'm going ___ Europe tomorrow.

4) There have been many wars ___ the last century. (a century = 100 years)

5) The snow was melted ___ the sun.

6) My glasses fell ___ (my face).

7) Please wait here. The doctor will be right ___ you. (will see you soon)

8) (At the store:) Do you have these shoes ___ black?

9) I think there's something wrong ___ my phone.

10) The town should be ___ that hill.

11) His speech was ___ morality.

12) I'm sorry ___ eating the last cookie.

13) This book was written ___ the 2nd century C.E. (C.E. means after Jesus' birth)

14) ___ his tone (of voice), I'd say he's not happy.

15) I dream ___ her every night.

16) (While flying:) I saw my house ___ the plane!

17) This cat weighs ___ fifteen pounds! (6.8 kilograms)

18) I don't know if we can complete the project ___ such stressful conditions.

19) I graduated university ___ two years ago.

20) I'll be there ___ 9:30.

21) He wrote a book ___ short stories.

22) I'm sorry, Mr. Johnson is ___ a meeting right now.

23) (In the gym:) He lifted the weights ___ his head.

24) The woman ___ the big coat is my sister.

25) He promised ___ take me home before 10 (PM).

Answers and Explanations

1) Here are some techniques **for** learning a language faster.

FOR: What do you want to do? What's the purpose or desired end-point/outcome of your action? You want to learn a language and you want to learn it faster. So, the techniques are "for" the purpose of learning a language faster.

A note about "of": We would never say, "some techniques of learning a language". However, you can say, "some language learning techniques", which is usually the other way to say it instead of using the preposition "of".

A note about "to": The preposition "to" works perfectly well, but the verb is in the "-ing" form, so it's not a correct answer. But that doesn't really matter, so that's why this note is here. So, if you say, "Here are some techniques to learn a language faster", it means the same thing. We're using "in order to", but this sentence is actually short for "Here are some techniques that you can use (in order) to learn a language". If we don't say "that you can use", then using "in order" sounds weird, but the idea is still there in the background either way.

2) The dog hid **under** the table.

UNDER: This is the most basic meaning of the preposition "under", which is usually the same as the preposition "below". This uses part two of the logic ("lower than or less than"). Note that the prepositions "beneath" and "underneath" can also work here, but they're very old and we don't use them as often as the prepositions "under" and "below".

3) I'm going **to** Europe tomorrow.

TO: Europe is your destination, which is a type of end point.

4) There have been many wars **over/in** the last century. (a century = 100 years)

OVER: In the main book, we saw the sentence, "I'll be in Japan over the winter". This is the same.

IN: Of course, a century is a large period of time that can be a container, so we can also use the preposition "in". However, the preposition "over" sounds a little better here.

5) The snow was melted **by** the sun.

BY: This is passive voice and it comes from group one in the main book, which is "an abstract medium that's a cause/source", or you can put it in group two ("mode/method (more specific versions of "way"); a concrete (not abstract) medium").

A note about "in": If you change the sentence to active voice, it would be: "The sun melted the snow" or "The snow melted in/under the sun". In this case, "in the sun" is short for "in the heat of the sun".

6) My glasses fell **off (of)/from** my face.

OFF (of): When you wear glasses, we say that the glasses are on your face. We don't usually need to say "my/your/his face". We use the preposition "on" because the glasses sit on the surface of your face. If they fall and are not on your face anymore, then they fell off. Again, we don't usually need to say "my/your/his face": "My glasses fell off".

FROM: Because we're using the verb "to fall", we can also use the preposition "from". If something falls, it starts falling from a certain point/place, so your face is the start point.

7) Please wait here. The doctor will be right **with** you. (will see you soon)

WITH: The logic of the preposition "with" is "together". You're waiting to see the doctor, so he/she is not with you right now. When the doctor is ready to see you, your name is called and you join the doctor in a room so that he can address your problems.

8) (At the store:) Do you have these shoes **in** black?

IN: This is the special group of "color, size, shape". Remember that with this group, we're usually not talking about the container itself, but the color, size, or shape of the container. In this case, you can also think of it this way: the color black "covers" the shoe, in which case the color can be the container.

9) I think there's something wrong **with** my phone.

WITH: There's a sentence in the main book: "We're having problems with our son." We also saw the sentence, "I'm having problems with my computer". This is the same as those sentences. Something is wrong and the problem is related to the phone, so the problem and the phone are "together".

10) The town should be **over/around/up/down/on/by** that hill.

OVER: "Over that hill" means "on the other side of that hill". This works because (in order) to reach the town, we have to go up one side and down the other side.

AROUND: "Around that hill" can have two meanings. 1) Similar to "by"/"close to". 2) "On the other side of that hill". The difference between using the preposition "around" and "over" in this case is that we can reach the other side by either going up one side and down the other ("over") or we can go around the hill and not go onto it at all.

UP: "Up that hill" means that the town is located on top of the hill, or it starts at the top of the hill. This is the basic use of the preposition "up" as an "upward direction" or an "upward position".

DOWN: This is the opposite of the preposition "up". The town is located at the bottom of the hill, or it starts at the bottom of the hill. This is a "downward direction" or a "downward position".

ON: This means "on top of" because a hill is a surface, and it can also be a kind of "platform" because it's raised.

BY: This means "near" and to the side.

11) His speech was **about/on** morality.

ABOUT: We know that books can be about or on a certain topic. Speeches work the same way. This is the same as the sentence that's in the main book, "This is a book about Gandhi".

ON: This is the same as the sentence that's in the main book, "This is a book on Gandhi".

12) I'm sorry **for/about** eating the last cookie.

FOR: The preposition "for" is the most basic answer here. We know that the logic of the preposition "for" is usually either a purpose or a basis. Which one are we using in this sentence? We're using the idea of a "basis". You ate the cookie. Based on that fact, you're apologizing, maybe because you feel bad.

ABOUT: We can also use the preposition "about", which is a little strange. Depending on the exact context, the preposition "for" or "about" might be more common, but they both usually work when you say sorry for something. Note that if you say "I apologize for", we don't say "I apologize about", probably because the word "apologize" sounds a little more formal and using the preposition "about" sounds more informal in this context.

But how does the logic of the preposition "about" apply here? We know that the logic is the idea of a "scope". If you're sorry about something, that thing is the scope of your apology/why you feel sorry. For example, if someone says you stole money, but you didn't, you shouldn't feel sorry or apologize because you didn't do it. In the example sentence, I ate the last cookie. That's something I did, and so it's the scope of why I feel sorry.

13) This book was written **in/around/by/over/about** the 2nd century C.E. (C.E. means after Jesus' birth)

IN: Remember that the preposition "in" is about containers, so in this case we have a container of time. A century is simply a larger container than a year (month → year → century), so we still use the preposition "in".

AROUND: If we don't know exactly when the book was written, we can use the preposition "around" with the meaning of "approximately". This is actually short for "in around the 2nd century", which is the same as saying "in approximately the 2nd century".

BY: The preposition "by" in this context is similar to a deadline. Remember the sentence that we saw in the main book: "Turn in the report by Friday". However, in the context of when something was done, such as when a book was written, we're not talking about a deadline. Like with the preposition "around", we don't know exactly when the book was written, but it wasn't later than the 2nd century. In other words, maybe it was written in the 1st century C.E. or the 1st century B.C.E. (before Jesus' birth), for example. All we know for certain is that the book was not written after the 2nd century C.E.

OVER: If we use the preposition "over", it means that the process of writing the book lasted all or most of the 2nd century. In other words, it was a large book that took about 100 years to complete. The logic is the same as in "over the winter".

ABOUT: The preposition "about" can have two meanings here. 1) "Approximately", just like the preposition "around". Again, this is short for "in about the 2nd century". 2) The topic of the book is the 2nd century. It's possible to use the preposition "on", too, but notice that all of the previous answers are related to when the book was written, not what the book is about. This is because it's more common to use the preposition "in" and related prepositions of time when talking about centuries, so the preposition "on" sounds a little weird and it sounds better if you use the preposition "about" in this case.

14) **By/From** his tone (of voice), I'd say he's not happy.

Other options: Because the logic here can be so abstract, let's look at some alternatives first so that we understand the basic meaning. One option is: "Given his tone (of voice)". Another way to say that is: "Based on his tone (of voice)". In both of these cases, we're using the information that we have and making a conclusion that's based on that information. Let's say that you ask this person how they are and he says, "I'm great!", but the way that he says it is with a low tone, low energy, and without a smile. More specifically, he sounds sad. Even though he says that he's great, he doesn't sound like he's great. Note that this doesn't have to be something opposite of what the person says. This is just a particular example to help make the idea clear.

BY: So how does the logic of the preposition "by" apply here? Notice that we're not using passive voice, so you might think that this doesn't belong in group one in the main book, which often uses passive voice. However, there was a specific example in group one: "Mom, can I go to my friend's house?" "It's fine by me." Remember that group one is about "an abstract medium that's a cause/source". In the explanation for that example, we saw that based on the mother's perspective or opinion, it's ok to go to the friend's house. We can see that both "by" and "based on" work because we're talking about a source or cause. So, when we say "by his tone", that piece of information is the basis of our conclusion ("he's not happy"). (Note: of course, the mother wouldn't say, "It's fine based on me", because we simply don't say that here, but the logic is there. Notice, however, that we can say, "If you ask me, it's fine".)

FROM: We can also use the preposition "from", because the preposition "from" is about a start point or origin point. We're using certain information ("his tone") as a starting point. From that starting point, we can make a conclusion ("he's not happy").

15) I dream **about/of** her every night.

ABOUT: The preposition "about" is probably more common that the preposition "of" here, but this is an example of when these two prepositions are interchangeable. The preposition "about" is a "scope". Notice that the preposition "on" does not work here. If you say, "I dream on her every night", it sounds like you sleep on top of her as you dream about something else, so the logic of the preposition "on" applies differently in this case. But also remember that the idea of a "scope" and the idea of "focusing on something" are very closely related, and it's almost impossible to talk about one without the other. So, what does the dream focus on? "Her". What's the scope of the dream? In other words, what does the dream contain? "Her".

OF: The preposition "of" sounds a little bit more formal, probably because it makes the sentence sound like an older style. Notice that in the explanation for the preposition "about", I asked the question, "What does her dream contain?" Of course, the preposition "of" is about either a "part" or "content". My dream isn't part of her, so she's the content of my dream. We can see that in this context, the prepositions "about" and "of" overlap very naturally, which is supported by key words like "contain" and "content" because the idea of a "scope" can apply to both of these words.

IMPORTANT NOTE: Sometimes when the prepositions "about" and "of" overlap, the meaning is exactly the same. However, sometimes the meaning is slightly different. This is all based on the context. We'll see similar examples later in this book.

16) (While flying:) I saw my house **from/on** the plane!

FROM: Where was I when I saw my house? I was on the plane. I saw my house from that point.

ON: This is actually short for, "I saw my house while I was on the plane". Obviously, it doesn't mean that my house was on top of the plane. This is a very good example of why context is important. In the main book, we saw phrases like "on the bus". Remember that vehicles that have the purpose of transporting many people are like big platforms, so we don't usually use the preposition "in" and instead we use the preposition "on".

17) This cat weighs **over/about/around** fifteen pounds! (6.8 kilograms)

OVER: In this case, the preposition "over" means "more than".

ABOUT: In this case, the preposition "about" means "approximately".

AROUND: In this case, the preposition "around" means "approximately".

Note about UNDER: Of course, you can use the preposition "under" with the meaning of "less than", but in this sentence, you're surprised because of how heavy the cat is. So the preposition "under" doesn't work in this specific case.

18) I don't know if we can complete the project **under** such stressful conditions.

UNDER: The logic of the preposition "under" is often a "downward force", usually with the meaning of "restricting" in some way. When there's stress, we often talk about it as a weight that pushes down on you, which can restrict many things. For example, you might not be able to focus very well; you might feel sad or depressed, which lowers your progress and efficiency; and we can also look at things like deadlines as restrictions, which might cause the stress.

19) I graduated university **about/around/over/under** two years ago.

ABOUT: The preposition "about" here means "approximately".

AROUND: The preposition "around" here means "approximately".

OVER: The preposition "over" here means "more than".

UNDER: The preposition "under" here means "less than".

20) I'll be there **at/around/about/by** 9:30.

AT: This is the most basic answer because we're talking about a specific time of day.

AROUND: The preposition "around" here means "approximately". It's short for "at around".

ABOUT: The preposition "about" here means "approximately". It's short for "at about".

BY: This means "not later than". 9:30 is like the "deadline" or the end point and I'll be there either before 9:30, or at 9:30.

Note about OVER: You might think that we can use the preposition "over" with the meaning "more than", specifically "later than". "Later than" is one of the few specific versions of "more than" that we don't use with the preposition "over". Instead, we use the preposition "after".

21) He wrote a book **of/on/about** short stories.

OF: The short stories are the content of the book.

ON: If we use the preposition "on", it means that "short stories" is the topic of the book. For example, maybe it's a book on how to write short stories.

ABOUT: This is the same as the preposition "on".

Note about FROM: You might think that we can use the preposition "from" with the same meaning as the preposition "of" because when we talk about what something is made of, we can usually use both of these prepositions. The logic of the preposition "from" works here and if you think about it, it doesn't sound too bad. However, we don't use it. Why? Because of the specific context and verb. If you use the preposition "from" here, it sounds more like he <u>took</u> some short stories and put them together in one book <u>instead of</u> <u>writing</u> the short stories. Although the preposition "of" still sounds better, we can say something like, "He <u>made</u> a book <u>from</u> all of his short stories."

22) I'm sorry, Mr. Johnson is **in** a meeting right now.

IN: We use the preposition "in" here because a meeting is like a process, which is a type of container. If there's a meeting and you don't attend, you're not inside that process, so you're outside of the container.

23) (In the gym:) He lifted the weights **over** his head.

OVER: First, he's holding weights in his hands. Then, he raises his hands upward until the weights are at a higher position than his head, usually directly above. The meaning here is "above", which you can also use.

Note: Many prepositions are possible here, but none of them are very common except for the preposition "over". For example, he can lift the weights with his head (meaning "using"), but who does that?

24) The woman **in/with** the big coat is my sister.

IN: Of course, this is actually short for "The woman <u>who's in</u> the big coat..."You can be "in" a coat because it's clothing. Remember that we usually use the preposition "on" when we talk about clothing because clothes go on the surface of your body, but we can also look at them as containers depending on the context and how we're talking about it. Another way to say this is: "The woman with the big on is my sister", which of course means, "The woman who's wearing the big coat is my sister".

WITH: This can have two meanings. 1) She's holding the coat and not wearing it. 2) She's wearing the coat. The only way to know for sure is to look at her. In both of these cases, the idea is "having" because if she's wearing it, we can say that she <u>has</u> it on (another way to say "wearing"), and if she's holding it, she <u>has</u> it in her hands.

25) He promised **to** take me home before 10 (PM).

TO: The preposition "to" is the only possible in this sentence. In the main book, we talked a lot about how the preposition "to" works with verbs. Remember that when we have two verbs and the preposition "to" is between them, it's like a bridge between the two actions. He made a promise, which is action one. "Take me home (before 10)" is the second action. The promise points to the action of taking me home, so that's what the promise is.

Multiple Fill-in-the-Blanks

Instructions: Each sentence has two or more blank spots. Fill in the blanks with the correct prepositions. There might be more than one correct answer.

Some of these are extremely difficult, and sometimes even native speakers might have trouble. This is because prepositions are part of the core of the English language and they help to give us clear contexts. Don't worry too much. Do your best and use the explanations in the answers section to help you understand things better. The purpose of this exercise isn't to get the correct answer, but to get accustomed to how multiple prepositions are applied in a single sentence depending on the context.

NOTE: Sometimes there's more than one right answer because sometimes prepositions are interchangeable or because it depends on the context. The preposition that you choose can sometimes change the context of the whole sentence.

1) (Calling the doctor's office:) Sorry. We're not allowed ___ give ___ patient data ___ the phone.

2) I went ___ the United States ___ the summer ___ 2009.

3) The proposal ___ build a new school is ___ consideration. (being considered)

4) I've been stuck ___ home ___ a broken leg.

5) I'm selling this lamp ___ $10, but I'll give (it to) you (for) a dollar ___ . (a $1 discount)

6) People gathered ___ the street musician ___ listen ___ his music.

7) ___ the age ___ ten, he had a strong interest ___ dinosaurs.

8) He likes ___ show ___ his skills. (Do things in a way that people will watch and think he's cool)

9) The bills are due ___ the end ___ the month.

10) The puppet is held ___ ___ wires.

11) He was ___ ___ go ___ bed when someone knocked ___ the door.

12) Next week, my son will be ___ ___ college. (Leaving home (in order) to go to college)

13) ___ Monday morning, we'll go ___ the details ___ the new assignment ___ depth.

14) "I get paid $10 per hour." "___ only $10 per hour, you'll barely be able ___ pay rent!"

15) ___ that point, he hadn't gone ___ ___ work ___ a week.

16) The plane took ___ ___ full speed.

17) Because I was sick __ a week, I have a lot __ work __ catch __ __.

18) We looked __ __ the ocean __ the hill.

19) I have you __ __ January 5th. (something that's already scheduled)

20) (Child to parent:) Can I go __ __ my friend's house?

Answers and Explanations

1) (Calling the doctor's office:) Sorry. We're not allowed **to** give (**out**) patient data **on/over** the phone.

TO: We saw information about "allowed to" in the main book. The idea is permission + to + give, so the preposition "to" connects the first action to the second action.

OUT: The preposition "out" is optional in this case. Remember that the preposition "out" is one of the prepositions that we like to use even when we don't need it, as long as the logic works and we get the same meaning. In this case, the preposition "out" changes the feeling of the verb "to give" a little. "Give out" can sound like you're giving something out to anyone and it doesn't matter who they are (this is a general "outward direction"). Even if the person calling is the patient, the doctor's office wants to make sure that they don't accidentally give patient information to the wrong person, so they have a policy that says that the people who work at the doctor's office can't give that information to anyone, even the patient.

ON: The preposition "on" is the most basic answer here. When we're talking about using the phone, the preposition "on" should always work or almost always work. In the main book, we saw the sentence, "She's talking on the phone". The logic is the same in this sentence.

OVER: We know that when we're talking about communications systems, there are many prepositions that we can possibly use, but the context and verb can restrict those options. For example, "She's talking on the phone". In that sentence, we can't use the preposition "over" because "talking on the phone" is more about the <u>active</u> process of using the phone, but "over the phone" is more about just using the phone as a tool and isn't focused on that process. It's a small difference and it just depends on what exactly you want to say. But when we specifically talk about giving information over the phone, the preposition "over" works because you're transferring that information through the phone instead of just

77

having a conversation about something. In the context of giving patient data to someone, compared to the preposition "on", the preposition "over" can give us a little extra feeling of "through the phone as a medium for transferring information".

The reason that the logic works here is because we're using the communications systems and the voices on both ends have to travel from one point all the way over to the other point (group two in the main book). You can call someone next door, in which case the distance is short, but normally when you call someone they're far enough away that you can't just go talk to them in person, so you use the communications systems to "carry" your voice over to them. Just remember, the preposition "over" won't always work, but it is possible to use the preposition "over" with "the phone" as long as it works in the context, which is partially based on the verb.

Note about BY: It is possible to use the preposition "by" in this sentence. However, there's a problem. We can't use the word "the": "by phone", not "by the phone". "By the phone" sounds like "close to the phone". Because of this, "by" is not an answer because we have the word "the", which we need when we use the other prepositions.

2) NOTE: This one is complicated because of all (of) the possibilities. (In order) to make it less confusing, I decided to create multiple parts because some answers don't work unless you change or remove another preposition. This might seem like a lot, but you'll see that it's not.

A) I went **to** the United States **in/for/by/over/around** the summer **of** 2009.

TO: The US is the destination, which is an end point.

IN: This is the most basic answer. Remember that when we talk about months, the container of time is so large that we're inside of it, so we use the preposition "in".

OF: A year has four seasons: spring, summer, fall, and winter. Each of these seasons are big "parts" of the year. In this case, the year 2009 is the total time (one year), and we're talking specifically about the part of 2009 that we call the summer.

FOR: We have some other options that we can use instead of the preposition "in". If we use the preposition "for", we're using part three of the logic, which is the special part that means "distance" or "duration". In this case, it's "duration" because we're talking about time. Notice that if we change the word "summer" to "three months", we can say, "I went to the United States <u>for three months</u> (in 2009; not 'of')". The only difference when use the word "summer" is that we're specifically labeling the three months so that it becomes one unit of time in which the weather is hot instead of just any three months sometime during the year (for example, February, March, and April).

BY: In this case, the preposition "by" means "not later than". You might be more likely to use the preposition "by" in this context if you can't remember exactly when you went to the US, but you know that it wasn't later than the summer of 2009.

OVER: This is the same as the example about "over the winter". It emphasizes that you spent the whole summer, or at least most of the summer, in the US.

AROUND: This use of the preposition "around" is a little special. If you say, "around the summer of 2009", we're not talking about the summer itself. Because the summer is such a large amount of time, we're talking about the time between spring and summer or the time between summer and fall (autumn). In other words, the meaning of the preposition "around" in this case is "approximately". You don't remember if it was in the summer, shortly before the summer, or shortly after the summer, so you're using the summer as a specific reference point (in order) to say that it was either close to summer or sometime during summer but you're not sure.

Note that this <u>does not</u> mean and <u>cannot</u> mean "surrounding" the summer, meaning the entire time. Instead, the specific point that we're surrounding with an abstract circle (part one of the logic) and/or the general "area" (time) of a specific point (part three of the logic) is the time between the seasons or some unknown time during summer. The specific point in time is the summer, but we're not talking about the summer itself.

B) I went **to** the United States **in/for/over/around** the summer **in** 2009.

IN #2: There are only two small differences between this group of answers and the previous group of answers. First, instead of the preposition "of" before "2009", we're using the preposition "in". This is just another way to look at a year. When we use the preposition "of", we're talking about the summer as a season that's part of the whole year. When we use the preposition "in", we're talking about the summer as being inside the year. Remember: "at 9:00", "on Monday", "in July", "in the summer", "in 2009", etc... A season is a large amount of time that's inside a larger amount of time (a year), so we can use the preposition "in".

However, there's one important thing to know about this. If you say, "in the summer", we like to say, "of 2009". This is because we have "in" and then "in" again when we have another option ("of"), so it can sound repetitive. The preposition "of" is also simply more common when talking about the month/season and the year in the same sentence, but the preposition "in" works perfectly fine here.

The second difference between this group of answers and the previous group of answers is that we can't use the preposition "by" before "the summer" because we're using the preposition "in" before "2009". These two prepositions simply don't work well together in this sentence. Why? If you say, "I went to the United States by the summer in 2009", it sounds like "the summer" is something that you can be physically next to. The logic still works, but this combination makes the surface meaning of the preposition "by" seem like it's from a different group.

80

C) I went **around** the United States **in/for/by/over** the summer **of** 2009.

AROUND: Notice that instead of the preposition "to" we have the preposition "around", but almost all (of) the other prepositions are the same as the first group of answers. There's only one difference: we can't use the preposition "around" before "the summer". First, we have to understand what the preposition "around" means when we say, "I went/traveled around the United States". This is exactly the same as saying, "I went/traveled around the city" or "I went/traveled around the world". As you can see, the verb "to go" ("went") and the verb "to travel" are interchangeable in this case. So why can't we use the preposition "around" again before "the summer"? Mostly because it sounds very repetitive.

Note about OVER: It's also possible to use the preposition "over": "I went all over the United States..." Notice that we have to use the word "all" here. The meaning in this case is the same as using the preposition "around" in the same place. Notice that this cannot mean "from one side to the other". You can use over that way, but it's not the meaning in this context. For example, "I went from California over to New York". Id you just say, "I went over the United States...", it sounds like "above". So maybe if you fly from Europe, over the US, and to another country, all without stopping in the US, then it can work.

D) I went **around** the United States **in/for/over** the summer **in** 2009.

In this last group of answers, everything is the same as the previous group, except now we're using the preposition "in" instead of the preposition "of" and because of that, we can't use the preposition "by" again. All of these answers have been explained in the previous groups.

81

3) The proposal **to** build a new school is **under** consideration. (being considered)

TO: Obviously this is the only answer here because the verb is not in the "-ing" form. But how does the logic work? Remember that when there are two actions/verbs and we use the preposition "to" (in order) to connect them, we usually have to talk about the first verb as a noun that points to the second verb. For example, in the sentence, "I want to leave", I have a desire that points to the action of leaving. The word "proposal" is a noun and the verb is "to propose". So in this case, the first verb is already in the noun form and that noun points to the action of building a new school. What's the goal (end point) of the proposal? "Build a new school".

Notice that we can change this a little and say, "I propose to build a new school". We can see that this works like "want to", "allow to", etc… There's another way to say that, which is, "I propose that we build a new school". The reasons for this are grammar and the type of verb, so it's important to know that sometimes we might not use the preposition "to" (in order) to point to the second action because we have other structures in those cases, particularly when we use the subjunctive mood, which has been slowly disappearing from English.

UNDER: The logic of the preposition "under" is a "downward force", often with the specific meaning of "restricting". The verb "to consider" means that you're going to think about something and all (of) its details. In this case, there's a new school. Things to consider include: Is it needed? How much will it cost? How will we pay for it? How big should the school be? Etc…

This process of consideration and decision making creates a "downward" force that will have a result: Don't build the school or build the school, and if you do build the school, what are all of the exact details? The verb is a little different, but this sentence is almost exactly the same as the sentence that we saw in the main book: "The terms of the contract are under

82

discussion". The logic works the same in both of these sentence.

4) I've been stuck **at** home **with** a broken leg.

AT: The verb "to stick" in this context means that you can't leave. It's similar to the general idea of the verb. For example, you can stick tape to the wall and it will stay there. We're using the preposition "at" in this sentence because we're talking about the location that I can't leave. I'm at home, but I can't leave.

WITH: The preposition "with" means "together". The specific meaning in this case is "having". My leg is broken. Another way to say that is, "I have a broken leg". So, I'm stuck at home. Why? Because I have a broken leg. "Stuck at home" + "have a broken leg" are together, which = "stuck at home with a broken leg".

Notice that we cannot say, "I'm with a broken leg". It's very important to remember that we can't always use the preposition directly because the prepositions are based on the context, which includes the specific verb that is used. The way we say this is, "I have a broken leg", but one of the surface meanings of the preposition "with" is "having". Sometimes the two are interchangeable, but they're obviously not the same thing. "Having" is simply one specific meaning of the preposition "with", but that doesn't mean that we can use the preposition "with" anytime that we want to express the idea of "having".

5) I'm selling this lamp **for** $10, but I'll give (it to) you (for) a dollar **off**. (a $1 discount)

FOR: When we have an exchange, we trade one basis for another basis. In this case, the first basis is a lamp and the second basis is ten dollars.

OFF: In this sentence, the preposition "off" means that we're removing something. Specifically, we're removing $1 from the total price of the lamp, so it only costs $9. How does the logic work here? It works exactly like the sentence that we saw in the main book: "Everything in the store is (on sale for) 50% off. (a 50% discount)".

6) People gathered **around/about/by** the street musician **to** listen **to** his music.

    Note: Notice that the person who's playing music is called a "street musician". This means someone that plays music outside, usually on the sidewalk. We say "street" because the person is outside while they play and because the goal is usually to get money from people who are walking by. If we were talking about a street instead of a street musician, there are other prepositions that we would be able to use, such as "in the street", "up the street", and "down the street". Because a "street musician" is a person, we can't use those prepositions here. Just don't get confused by the word "street" because it's actually part of the term "street musician".

    AROUND: The verb "to gather" means that people or things are brought together in some way. If people gather, it means that many people are coming into the same area. The preposition "around" in this case means that the street musician is in the center and the people are standing around him in a circle, meaning that the people form the shape of the circle. This can also be a semi-circle.

    ABOUT: The preposition "about" also works here, but it sounds more British or older.

    BY: In this case, there might be a circle, but probably not. The preposition "by" in this case simply means "close to".

    TO: The first preposition "to" in this sentence is short for "in order to". Why are they gathering? What's the purpose of it? So that they can listen to the music.

    TO: This is the most basic and most common preposition here. The verb "to listen" very often uses the preposition "to", but why? We have two verbs: "to listen" and "to hear". Hearing is more passive because sounds just enter your ears. You can hear something, but you might not be focused on it. Listening is more active because you're focusing your attention on something. It's kind of like "active hearing".

So, you're actively directing your attention/focus to the sounds that you hear. In other words, the sounds – or in this case, the music – is the end point.

Note about FOR: The preposition "for" in this context isn't common. In fact, in this specific sentence, it doesn't work. However, this is a good example of the differences between the prepositions "to" and "for". If you listen for something, it means that you don't hear it now, but you're focusing your attention and concentrating (in order) to try to hear some sound that you're expecting. For example, let's say that you go to the doctor's office and check in. The person who checks you in says, "Take a seat and listen for your name to be called". The logic of the preposition "for" in this case is a "purpose".

7) **From/At/By/Around/About** the age **of** ten, he had a strong interest **in** dinosaurs.

FROM: "From the age of ten" simply means "starting at the point in time when he was ten years old".

AT: "At the age of ten" means that when he was ten, he had that interest. Maybe he also had the interest before and/or after the age of ten, but we're only talking about when he was ten. This is clearly a specific point. Imagine a line with numbers on it that starts at 0 (birth) and ends at 20, for example. We're talking about the specific point that's at the number 10.

BY: "By the age of ten" means that he developed the interest no later then the age of ten. He might have had the interest before that, but we don't know. All we know for certain is that starting as late as ten years old, he had that interest.

AROUND: This means "approximately" and is short for "at around".

ABOUT: This means "approximately" and is short for "at about".

OF: Note that "ten" is short for "ten years old". We use the preposition "of" here because "ten years old" is the content of "age". Specifically, it's the number of years that he's been alive, so the content is an amount. It's much more common to use amounts as parts (for example, five pieces of pizza), but remember that there are some cases in which either part of the logic of the preposition "of" can apply in the opposite direction.

IN: Remember that the preposition "in" is a one-way preposition, but there are some rare cases in which the logic can go the opposite direction. When we talk about interests, it's one of these rare cases, but you can look at it both ways: either he put interests into a container called "dinosaurs" or he put dinosaurs into a container called "interests". You can choose whichever one is easier to understand and remember.

8) He likes **to** show **off** his skills.

TO: This is just like "want to". In this case, he has a like, and that like points to the action of showing off. Here, we can't just say that it points to "showing" because "show off" is a phrasal verb, meaning that it's one idea, like a two-word verb.

OFF: So what does the phrasal verb "show off" mean and how does the logic work? "Show off" means that someone shows other people that they're really good at something, usually so that they can brag about it. The verb "to brag" basically means "I'm so great because I can do this thing!" These two ideas ("show off" and "brag") are very closely related, but "to brag" means that you're <u>talking about</u> the thing (notice that we say "<u>brag about</u> something") and "show off" means that you're actually doing/showing the thing.

But how does the logic of the preposition "off" work here? This phrasal verb has a feeling of "outward direction" or "<u>away from a center point</u>" (group three of the preposition "off" in the main book). Remember, the prepositions "on", "off", "up", "down", and "out" are very closely related and sometimes things get messy. The idea here is that you are your central platform (more information in group five of the preposition "down" in the main book). From that central platform, you want to get attention. You want people to look at you and say, "Wow! That's cool!" So you perform like you're

86

an actor on a stage and you're trying to send a "message" outward to anyone who will notice. That message says, "Hey, look at me!"

9) The bills are due **at/by/about/around** the end **of** the month.

AT: This is the most basic answer. "At the end of the month" means on the 30th/31st. However, remember that the preposition "at" also uses the abstract "bubble" idea, as well as the "target" idea, so there's often a little bit of extra space or time around the specific point, depending on the context. So, "at the end of the month" might include the days from the 28th of the first month to the 3rd of the next month, but the focus is the last day of the month.

But if we're talking about days of the month, why don't we say, "On the end of the month"? In this case, the context tells us that we're talking about days, but what we're actually talking about is the end of the month. A month is a period of time, and like all periods of time, there's a beginning and an end. These are two specific points in time when something starts and stops.

BY: "By the end of the month" means "not later than the end of the month". It is possible to include a few days after the end of the month, but this really sounds like a deadline, so the emphasis is more on the last day of the month. Of course, you can pay the bills before then because the preposition "by" with this meaning includes the time before it until the point where we reach the end.

ABOUT: This means "approximately" and is short for "at about". The reason this can work is because now we're not saying that the bills are due on the last day of the month, but close to that day. Maybe on the 5th, for example. The number of days that are covered is a little more than with the preposition "at".

AROUND: This means "approximately" and is short for "at around". All the details are the same as for the preposition "about" in the previous explanation.

OF: The end of the month is <u>part</u> of the month. A month has a beginning, a middle, an end, and other things, like a name ("the name of the month"), which we usually don't talk about and just say "September", for example. All of these things are parts of what we call a "month".

10) The puppet is held **up/out** **by/with** wires.

UP: If you hold something up, it means that you hold it in a way that it is raised, meaning an upward position. In this case, wires are attached to a puppet's arms and legs and you pull the wires upward so that the puppet is standing instead of laying down on the ground. After you pull the wires upward, you can <u>hold the wires</u> at that height so that the puppet stays standing, so we say that the puppet is held up.

OUT: The preposition "out" can also work, but now the wires are very strong and you're holding the puppet out in front of you using the wires. This is simply a direction that is outward from your body or from whatever the wires are attached to.

BY: Notice that this sentence uses passive voice, so the preposition "by" is very natural here. This belongs to group one in the main book, which is "an abstract medium that's a cause/source"??? What's the <u>way</u> that the puppet is held up? In other words, how is the puppet held up? By wires.

WITH: The meaning of the preposition "with" here is "using". The wires are attached to the puppet, so they are together. If you move the wires, the puppet will move, too.

11) He was **about** **to** go **to** bed when someone knocked **on/at/down** the door.

ABOUT: Remember that "about to" is special because we're combining the logic of the prepositions "about" and "to". The logic of the preposition "about" is a "scope". There's the point in time when he goes to bed and the point in time right before that. The scope is centered around these two points (in order) to show that they're close to each other. Remember, this is the idea of "almost", but we don't say, "He was almost to go to bed". Instead, we use the preposition "about". This is from group four in the main book.

TO: The preposition "to" points to the verb "to go" as an end point and connects the preposition "about" with the verb "to go". The preposition "about" then puts the present moment (or the moment that we're talking about: "He was") into the same scope of time as the action of going.

TO: The second preposition "to" seems to be pointing to the destination (end point) of where he was going. In this case, it's "bed". In this particular case, however, we have something a little strange because "go to bed" is one phrase that means "go to sleep" and not "go to the location of the bed" because people usually sleep in beds. So, we simply use this as another way to express the same idea. What we're really saying here is "go to sleep", so the preposition "to" is really connecting the first action to the second action.

ON: A door is a surface, which means that it's something that you can hit. When I knock on the door, the surface of my fingers hit the surface of the door.

AT: You can think of the door as a target, but that doesn't always work. For example, we don't say, "He knocked at the table". Instead, we say, "He knocked on the table". So how does the preposition "at" work here if the door isn't a target? It's a strange one, but we can use it because someone is standing at the door (a specific point, which is the entry to the building or room) when they knock, so we can just combine these two ideas ("standing at the door" + "knock") and say "knock at the door".

DOWN: If someone knocks down a door, it means that they kick it, push themselves into it, or use some other kind of force (in order) to make a locked door open. This can cause the door to completely disconnect from the wall and fall to the ground (which is where we get the idea of "down"), but often it just breaks in some way.

12) Next week, my son will be **off to/at** college. (Leaving home (in order) to go to college)

89

OFF: Do you remember the sentence "I'm off to work" (not "I'm off of work")? This sentence was in group four in the main book. The meaning of that group is: "starting to move away from a central point". Remember that the "central point" is like an abstract platform, so depending on the context, we can also call it a "central platform". It's usually wherever you are now or whatever place that you're thinking about, and it's very often your house because that's like the central location where you exist in life. When you leave home (in order) to go to work, you're removing yourself from the central platform so that you can begin the action/process of working. The meaning that we get from this is "I'm leaving (in order) to go to work", which is the start of your journey to the place that you work.

It works the same way in the sentence, "My son will be off to college". Let's say that he's eighteen years old and he's going to be living at the college as he studies there. So, he's going to start college and we're specifically talking about him leaving (in order) to do that. Note that if someone goes to college but they continue living at home while they attend, they don't go "off to college" because they still live at home, meaning that they're not leaving the central platform. They temporarily leave (in order) to go to class, but they're not really leaving because they come back home every night.

TO: "College" is the destination, which is an end point. In this case, it's their "permanent" destination for the next 4+ years because they'll be living there, so in this specific context there's a little bit of extra meaning in the background.

AT: "Off at college" is a little different than "off to college", and it makes perfect sense. "Off to college" means that we have a location and we're emphasizing going to that location, which is the destination (end point). "Off at college" emphasizes the location itself and not the location as a place to go to (destination). In the specific context of going to college, the preposition "to" sounds like he's starting college, but "at college" just sounds like that's where he'll be, especially if

90

we're saying that that's where he'll be during something else that's happening in another location.

13) **On/Over** Monday morning, we'll go **over** the details **of** the assignment **in** depth.

ON: The day of the week is like a platform and/or it's the "active" day.

OVER: This isn't a common answer in this case, but it's definitely possible. This is the same as the idea that we find in the phrase "over the winter". If we say "over Monday morning", it means that we're going to be doing something for all or most of that morning. This also means that there are a lot of details that we're going to discuss, because it will take all or most of the morning (in order) to complete that process.

OVER: The phrasal verb "go over" means "to review" or "to analyze". The verb "to go" creates motion. We're obviously not going anywhere physically, but because we're going to be talking about the details, it's like we're moving through the details. The preposition "over" in this case can work two ways. The second option is better, but it's based on the first option: 1) if you're looking at the details on paper, your eyes are literally looking at the page from above as you go through the details (group one in the main book); 2) you're going through the details and discussing/analyzing them starting from the top of the page to the bottom or the page; or if there's no paper, then you're going through the details from the first point in the discussion to the last point in the discussion. This is an abstract application of group two from the main book (from one side of something to the other side (above + movement)). If the details are on paper, then the first "side" is the top of the page/document and the second "side" is the bottom of the page/document. Notice that we can also use the words "start" and "end" instead of the words "top" and "bottom".

OF: An assignment might be homework or a project, for example. The assignment has details, so those details are part of the assignment.

IN: We know that the preposition "in" is about a "container". In this case, if we try to separate the words "in" and "depth", it doesn't work very well because this a chunk. "Depth" is the noun form of the adjective "deep" and it isn't the container itself. Instead, "depth" is a part of a container. How deep is the container?/What's the depth of the container?

When we do something "in depth", it means that we're not just doing a little bit. We're going deep into that action or topic/subject. For example, if you're studying English and you want to be an advanced speaker, you have to go very deep into the language so that you can learn all or most of the details. Or if you're getting a degree in psychology, then you want to become an expert, so you have to read and learn a lot about it. This means that you're going deep into the subject of psychology.

So, the assignment has details. We're not just going to list those details or quickly mention them. Instead, we're going to analyze the details, ask and answer questions about it, etc... so that everyone completely understands what the details are and what everyone has to do (in order) to complete the assignment. We're going deep into the details, so the details are the container.

14) "I get paid $10 per hour." "**At** only $10 per hour, you'll barely be able **to** pay rent!"

AT: If I get paid $10 per hour, then that is the rate at which I get paid. A rate can be a form of measurement. How often and how much are both amounts that we can use as measurements. Remember that we can use the preposition "at" (in order) to talk about a specific amount, which can be a point on a scale of measurement.

TO: Here we have "be able" + "to" + "pay" (verb 1 + to + verb 2). So we're talking about an ability and the preposition "to" points to the action of paying, meaning that it connects the two ideas.

15) **At/By** that point, he hadn't gone (**in/up/down/over/out/off**) **to** work **for/in** a week.

AT: We're talking about a specific point in time, so we can use the preposition "at" in this case.

BY: This is the same as the preposition "at", except we're saying that it might have happened sooner, but definitely not later than that point in time.

IN: This is the most basic answer. When we say "go in to work", it means leaving home and going to your job. Because your job isn't at home and you have to enter a different building, we can use the preposition "in". You can also think of this as starting the process of working, but only if it's away from home. Both buildings and processes can be containers. Notice that this preposition and all the other prepositions that can replace it are optional because we can simply say, "he hadn't gone to work".

UP: If we use the preposition "up", it feels like one of the following possibilities: 1) his work is at a physically higher location, like on a hill; 2) his work is located in a northward direction (but the distance has to be far enough; if he works next door and next door is north from where he was, we don't use the preposition "up" because it's too close)

DOWN: If we use the preposition "down", it's exactly the same as the preposition "up", but the opposite (physically lower location or southward direction).

OVER: If we use the preposition "over", it's similar to the prepositions "up" and "down". We know that the preposition "over" can mean "eastward" or "westward", so if we use that meaning, it's the same as the previous two prepositions. The other meaning of the preposition "over" in this case is simply "over there". The preposition "over" in this case isn't very common compared to the other prepositions.

OUT: If we use the preposition "out", it sounds like he has to go a long distance, but particularly outside of the city, or if he lives in the countryside and has to leave that (in order) to go into the city. Either way, he's going out of the container of the city or the container of the country side.

93

OFF: This preposition is also less common in this context, but it's the same as the preposition "off" in the sentence, "I'm off to work". The person who says "he hadn't gone off to work" probably lives with him because the person is speaking/thinking from the perspective of being at home, which is the central platform in this case.

TO: "Work" in this case isn't a verb, it's a noun. We're simply talking about the place where he works. So "work" is the destination, which is an end point.

FOR: The preposition "for" in this case is about the length of time. This is part three of the logic ("distance/duration").

IN: We can also use the preposition "in" here. Remember that when we talk about doing something in a certain amount of time, we're saying that the action happens in that period of time, but we're specifically focused on the end result. If I say, "I'll be home in two days", it means that at the end of two days, I'll be home. It does not mean that I'll be home sometime before that. We use the preposition "within" for that. Another example: "The food will be done cooking in ten minutes". It takes 10 minutes for the food to cook, so it won't be ready before that. In other words, the second day or the tenth minute is the container and that container holds the result (I'm home or the food is done cooking).

So when we say "in a week", it means that he hadn't worked for the entire week. At the end of that week, he still hadn't worked. After that, maybe he returned to work, but that's not the focus of this sentence. What's happening here is that "at the end of the week" becomes the container that holds the result. In other words, like being at a store or in a store, we're going inside the point that's at the end of the week. We'll see another example like this and talk about it more in another exercise.

94

16) The plane took **off** **at** full speed.

OFF: This is similar to the sentence, "I'm off to work". A plane can move on the ground when it's wheels are down, but obviously a plane is designed to fly. So, in order to leave, it has to start flying. The central platform for the plane is the airport because that's where planes "live", so we can apply the "starting to move away from a central point" idea. Of course, we can also apply the most basic meaning of the preposition "off", which is "removed from a surface/platform". The ground is a surface, and planes fly, so it literally moves off of the ground and into the sky.

Notice that the verb is very important here. You might want to use the preposition "up" because the plane flies upward and away from the ground. It's possible to use the preposition "up", but you have to change the sentence: "The plane flew up into the sky". When we use the verb "to take", we're looking at things from a different perspective. As the plane moves forward on the ground, the wheels are "taking" the ground, which moves it forward. As the plane starts to fly upward, the wings "take" the air and use it to rise upward.

AT: "Full speed" is a measurement of speed. In this case, we don't care exactly what that speed is. The important thing is that it's as fast as the plane can go before it starts flying, which is a specific point of measurement.

17) Because I was sick **for** a week, I have a lot **of** work **to** catch **up** **on**.

FOR: This means "duration"; it's the length of time that I was sick.

OF: When we say, "a lot of" something, you can look at it both ways: either as a part or as content. In the main book, we saw the sentence, "A lot of people are at the beach." The work is the content of the amount. A lot of what? Work. But each thing that I have to do for work is one piece of the total amount of work that I have to do.

TO: Another way to say this is "a lot of work that I have to catch up on". In that case, we're using the word "that" (in order) to define or describe the work. Is it work that I finished? Work that I'm doing now? No, it's work that I have to do/catch up on. Instead of using the word "that" and saying all of those extra words, we can simply use the preposition "to", which points directly to the verb. It's like a shortcut. Of course, as always, this also depends on the context (which includes if you change subjects or not ("I", "you", "he", etc…). You can't always replace "something that something" with the preposition "something to do", but we can see how and why it works here.

UP: The phrasal verb "catch up" means that your progress with something is not where it should be. Specifically, you're behind. In this sentence, I was sick for a week, which means that I didn't work for an entire week. (In order) to make things simple, let's imagine that I was working on a project. Before I was sick, I had completed 10% of the project. If I hadn't become sick, I would have worked on the project for the entire week. Let's say that after that week of work the project would have been 50% complete, but because I was sick, the project is still only 10% complete. So I have to work harder (in order) to complete the project on time. This is called "catching up". The project should be 50% completed right now, but it's not, so I have to catch up because of the time that I lost when I was sick.

Notice that we're using the verb "to catch". This verb has more than one meaning, but one of the meanings is "to grab something that's moving". In the phrasal verb "catch up", you're not physically catching something. Instead, you have to try to reach the point where you should be. In the context of this sentence, it's like time is moving away from you, which moves the point of progress where your project/work should be forward. But you're not actually working on it, so you have to work harder so that you can "catch" the point where your work should be.

And the preposition "up"? The meaning here is that you have to move forward to the point where you should be in your work. This is a "forward direction", but in time and/or

96

progress instead of in space. Imagine that someone is running faster than you and they're currently ahead of you. If you want to catch them, you have to run faster than they're running so that you can reach the point where they are. It's the same idea: you're behind, but if you work harder, you can get closer to the point that you need to reach so that you can finish the project/work on time.

ON: The preposition "on" here is the same as the preposition "on" in the sentence, "I'm working on a new book".

18) We looked **out** **over/to/at** the ocean **from** the hill.

OUT: because we're on a hill, we can see a lot. Our vision is going outward and we can see for a long distance.

OVER: The preposition "over" in this sentence can have two meanings. The basic meaning is "above" because we're on a hill and the ocean is at a lower position than we are. But we can also apply the idea of "from one side of something to the other side (above + movement)". We can use this meaning because we're not just looking outward. We see a lot of the ocean, so our vision goes outward <u>and</u> left and right. So "out over the ocean" is like saying "out <u>and</u> over the ocean".

TO: This is like saying, "Look to the sky". Remember that the focus isn't the sky ("Look at the sky"). The focus is usually either something that's in the sky or simply "upward". This is one of the cases where the preposition "to" includes the idea of a direction, but remember that the preposition "toward" is a direction and the preposition "to" is about an end point.

If we look out to the ocean, it means that the ocean is the direction and the end point is something else. Maybe you're looking for a ship, for example. Or it could just be generally "outward" in that direction with no specific end point, just like "look to the sky" can be upward with no specific end point. If there's no specific end point, then it's just whatever end points – if any – that you might see (ships, whales, etc...).

97

AT: If you look (out) at the ocean, it means that the focus is the ocean itself and something in the ocean or in the direction of the ocean.

FROM: We're on the hill. Starting at that point, we look outward. Our sight starts on the hill and extends out over the ocean.

19) I'm **under** the assumption that you're **in** charge **around** here, correct? (I think that you're the boss/manager)

UNDER: If you're under an assumption, it means that you assume something. It's the same as saying, "I assume...", but it sounds polite. An assumption is similar to a belief (except an assumption doesn't use the preposition "in", only "under"). In the main book we saw this sentence: "Many people are under the belief that human nature is bad." This is from group four of the preposition "under". When we say "under the assumption that...", the logic of the preposition "under" is the same.

IN: "In charge" is a chunk. If you're in charge, it means that you're the person who makes the decisions and tells other people what to do. For example, a manager is in charge of the employees that work under him or her. But why do we use the preposition "in" here? Are we making the word "charge" a container? Yes and no. Remember, "in charge" is a chunk. Chunks often work like one unit, almost like one multi-part word, so separating them and talking about the individual words is difficult sometimes. We saw this problem in the main book when we talked about the phrase "in order to". Luckily, "in charge" isn't as complicated as "in order to".

Notice that we can say that if someone is a manager, they're in a position of management. This is based on an older phrase that we still use: "in a position of power". This can apply to managers and other high level people in a company, high level government jobs like president or member of congress/parliament, or the head of a school, for example. So the word "charge" itself isn't the container. The position is the container and the word "charge" gives us the idea that the person has some power.

AROUND: The preposition "around" in this context uses the third part of the logic ("within the general area of a specific point"). Where exactly this point is depends on the context and location. For example, if they're the manager of a store, "around here" means "in this store".

20) I have you **down** **on /for** January 5th.

DOWN: This example is like the example that we saw in the main book about writing down an email address, but there's a slight difference. "To have someone down" means that the person scheduled something or made some sort of reservation, such as at a restaurant. Their name and other important details are written or stored somewhere for the purpose of reserving their spot.

For example, if I want to go to a fancy restaurant, I have to make a reservation. So I call the restaurant and the person on the phone writes my name, the day and the time that I'll be coming, and how many people will be coming with me. Another example: I forget what day and/or time my doctor's appointment is, so I call the doctor's office and ask. The person on the phone tells me, "I have you down for January 5th". So this is very similar to the email address example, but in this case, all of that information is written down and secured somewhere.

ON: January 5th is the day that's active for your appointment. For example, let's say that you have a doctor's appointment, but you forgot to write down what the specific day of the appointment is. You call the doctor's office and the person on the phone says, "I have you down on January 5th". That's the day when your appointment will happen/be active/exist. Of course, we can also just think of the calendar as a surface where my name is written.

FOR: We know that we use the preposition "on" with specific days of the week ("Monday", for example) and specific dates ("the 5th", for example). That's because whatever day/date it is that we're talking about, that's the active day/date. Although it's a little less clear, we've seen in the main book that we can also think of a day/date as an abstract platform. But we're talking about the preposition "for" here, so why am I talking about the preposition "on"? Because that abstract platform can become a "basis", which is the second part of the logic of the preposition "for". This is part of the underground/subconscious connections that a native speaker of English usually isn't aware of. But why does the idea of a basis work here? Because that's the date of your appointment, reservation, etc… It will happen on that day, so that day is the "support" of the event. If it's the fourth, then it doesn't happen. There's nothing to support it. There's no reason to go to your appointment or reservation because it's the wrong day. Based on the fact that it's the 5th, you can now go to the appointment or whatever it is that's scheduled.

Confusing Prepositions 2

Instructions: This exercise is will help you understand the differences between closely related prepositions more clearly. Each sentence has two or three choices. Choose the correct one. Sometimes, more than one is correct, but the context might change. Like before, if there are answers that are extremely unlikely, don't choose them.

1) Don't throw things <u>at / to / for</u> me!

2) I'm <u>in / on / at</u> the library.

3) Was this book written <u>by / of / about / from</u> you?

4) I know <u>of / about</u> him.

5) Can you turn the light <u>off / down / out</u>.

6) <u>In / At</u> the end, she had to do it alone.

7) Look <u>on / to / in / at</u> the car.

8) I used this computer <u>to</u> write my book. / I used this computer <u>for</u> writing my book.

9) There's one piece <u>to / about / of / from</u> this mystery that's missing.

10) Do you remember what the name <u>of / from</u> that song is?

11) I don't like the colors <u>in / of / on</u> this painting.

12) The size <u>in / of</u> this shirt is too big.

Answers and Explanations

1) Don't throw things **at** me!

AT: This is the best answer. If someone throws something at you, they're trying to hit a specific point, which is the space where you currently are. In other words, you're a target.

TO: Of course, this preposition can work, but it doesn't make much sense in this context. If I throw something to you, I want you to catch it because you're the end point. Why would you tell someone <u>not</u> to throw things to you?

FOR: This one can also work, but again, not in this context. If I throw something for you, it means that instead of you throwing it, I throw it so that you don't have to. This is the idea of exchanging one basis for another basis.

2) I'm **in / at** the library.

IN: If you're inside of the library, then the building is a container.

AT: If you're at the library, that's your current location. It's a specific point/"bubble". It doesn't matter if you're inside the library or outside the library as long as there's some reason that you're there. Remember that in cases like this, the preposition "in" is actually inside of the preposition "at", so if you're inside of the library, you can still use the preposition "at".

ON: This one also works, but it's extremely unlikely. This means that you're physically on top of the library (on the roof).

3) Was this book written **by / about** you?

BY: If you wrote the book, then the book was written by you. This is passive voice and it belongs to group one in the main book ("an abstract medium that's a cause/source").

ABOUT: If the book is about you, then you're the topic of the book. For example, maybe someone wrote your biography (a book that's about your life).

OF: In this specific context, the preposition "of" isn't a good choice. The logic works because you're the content of the book, but here it sounds like a very old way to say this sentence. However, there are other contexts where we still use the preposition "of" in a similar way. For example, "The people of this city speak of strange things that happen at night". This means that you if you go that city, you'll probably hear people talk about those strange things.

The chunks "speak of", "smell of" (more common: "smell like"), "taste of" (more common: "taste like"), "hear of" (usually "have heard of"), and "think of" are normal chunks, but the first three sound a little old and more formal. These are small, specific details that you can get accustomed to over time, so don't worry about mastering all of them now. Remember, we're trying to find the feeling of English prepositions through the logic, not learn every little random detail.

The point here is that the logic of the preposition "of" can apply to "written of", but we don't apply it here. However, there are some specific cases where we do still apply it. If you chose the preposition "of" as an answer, it's a good answer and it means that you're feeling the preposition, but unfortunately we don't use it in this specific sentence. This is all part of the learning process.

FROM: It's possible to use the words "written from" together, but not here. We can say that the book came from you, though that sounds like you sent me the book, so it's not about if you wrote it or not. An example of when we can say "written from" is: "This book was written from the perspective of a soldier in World War II". That doesn't mean that the soldier wrote the book, it means that as you read the book, you see the story through him. You see what he sees, hear what he hears, and you know his thoughts and feelings because you're inside his head.

4) I know **of / about** him.

OF: Both of these prepositions work! However, the meaning is slightly different. If you say, "I know of him", it sounds like you know that he exists, but nothing else.

ABOUT: If you say, "I know about him", it means that you know something about him. It might be just a little bit, like maybe you know that he's the author of a particular book or that he's a teacher. Or you might know more, like where he works, some things that he likes, etc… However, you haven't met him. You've gotten all of this information from other sources (online, from friends, etc…). After you meet, it means that you now "know" him, even if you don't know him very well.

You should know that there are some smaller details about usage here, but we won't talk about them.

5) Can you turn the light **off / out**.

OFF: The most basic answer here is the preposition "off". The light is on (positive state/active state) and I ask you to turn it off (negative state/inactive state).

OUT: We can also use the preposition "out". The preposition "off" and "out" are kind of similar, but in this case, the explanation is very simple. In the past, we didn't have electricity, but we did have candles. A candle isn't something that you "turn off" because there's no light switch. Instead, you have to put it out in some way (the most common is "blow out"). What probably happened is that the logic of the preposition "out" continued to be applied after we started using electricity, but now that there's a light switch, we can use the verb "to turn" and we get: "turn out".

Either way, you can see that the light is in the room (or shining into the room) and when you turn the light out/off, it's not in the room anymore.

DOWN: It's possible to say, "Turn the light down", but it's a lot less common. If you have a dimmer switch, you can make the light brighter or dimmer (less bright). In that case, you can use the preposition "down" with the meaning of "dimmer" (decreased brightness) and the preposition "up" with the meaning of "brighter" (increased brightness).

6) **In** the end, she had to do it alone.

IN vs AT: This is a common problem for many English learners, and the mistake isn't always with a preposition. For example, many Spanish speakers try to say "finally" in a sentence like this, and that doesn't work, either. So first, what does "in the end" mean? We're talking about the end result of something. Let's say that she wanted to paint her house and she doesn't have the money to pay someone to do it. She asked friends and family for help. Maybe some of them said that they would help, but no one did. So the result is that she had to do it alone. "Finally" is similar, but that word is more about doing something after some amount of time, usually after it was supposed to be done or after you wanted it to be done.

Ok, so how does the logic of the preposition "in" apply here and how does it create the meaning of a "result"? The end point ("at the end") becomes a container. The preposition "at" only talks about the specific point in time itself, like saying "at 9:00", or "at the store" if we're talking about a specific point in space. Usually, we can go into a specific point/location in space (like a store), but we can't go into a specific point in time. For example, what does "in 9:00" mean? Nothing. It doesn't make any sense. But certain words like the word "end" aren't just specific points in time. We can also use them as containers. So, using the phrase "at the end" as a basis, we can go inside that point (in order) to talk about the result. What happened at the end as a result of everything? Now we're inside that point and it's a container, just like you can go into a store. You're still "at the store", just like we're still "at the end", but we're specifically going into that point.

Remember the sentence that we saw earlier? "By that point, he hadn't gone in to work in a week". "In a week" focuses on the <u>result that's at the end</u> of that period of time. The point at the end is the container that holds the result. This is the same as "in a minute", "in a year", etc… Now we know that we can also use certain other words, like "in the <u>end</u>" and "in the <u>beginning</u>". If we talk about "in the beginning", obviously it's not a result because we're not combining the words "in" and "end". Instead, we're combining the words "in" and "beginning". Just like a phrasal verb combines a verb and a preposition (in order) to create a specific meaning, we can choose either the word "end" or "beginning" (in order) to get a specific meaning. "In the beginning" is about the state of things at the start of something, and that state is the container. You can see once again that the prepositions "in" and "on" are closely related.

Lastly, it's important to remember that there's usually more than one way to say the same thing. "In the beginning" is the same as "at first", but the context sometimes determines which one we can use. Remember, the prepositions "at", "on", and "in" are very closely related. Feeling them is a great start and will help you easily know which preposition to use in many cases, but it will take time to get accustomed to some of the phrases and contexts that use each one.

7) Look **on** / **in** / **at** the car.

ON: This is short for "look so that you can see what's on top of the car". That's the only possible meaning of the preposition "on" in this case, so we can simply say "on the car".

IN: This means that you're going to look inside of the car, either because you want to see something that's on the inside or because you're searching for something that's inside.

AT: The car is the focus, so it's the target of your vision. You're not looking at something that's on top of the car, inside of the car, around the car, etc... You're looking at the car itself.

TO: In this case, if you want to express the idea of "in the direction of the car", we have to use the preposition "toward". Why? Because the car isn't the end point of our vision. If we wanted to say that, we would say, "Look at the car" (remember that a "target" is a special kind of end point).

107

8) I used this computer **to** write my book.

TO: This is short for "in order to". I used the computer for the purpose of writing the book and so that I could write the book ("ability" + "purpose").

FOR: We're talking about a purpose, so obviously this isn't short for "in order for" because that can only be a basis. But sometimes it's still possible to use the preposition "for" by itself. It might be possible to say, "I used this computer for writing my book", but it sounds a little strange.

9) There's one piece **to / of** this mystery that's missing.

TO: Remember that there's a very specific case in which the prepositions "to" and "of" touch, or possibly overlap. This is when we're talking about pieces with a meaning that's similar to a puzzle. A mystery is similar to a puzzle because you have to find details/evidence about what's happening or what happened and then put those details together so that you can see the whole picture and solve the mystery.

The preposition "to" works because the mystery has many (abstract) pieces that you have to find and put together. Notice the word "together". It's actually, "to" + "gether". "Gether" isn't a word in Modern English, but it's related to the verb "to gather". When you gather all the pieces, you can put them to-gether. If there's one piece missing, then you have an almost completed "picture" of what happened. You need to find the last piece and add it to the whole. Like a puzzle, it goes in a certain spot, which I n this case means that it explains a certain thing about what happened. The spot that the piece fills – which includes it's connection to the whole – is the end point.

OF: We can also use the preposition "of" here. It works because each detail/piece of evidence is part of the mystery. More specifically, in this case they're part of solving the mystery, meaning part of the solution of the mystery.

ABOUT: When we're talking about pieces that are like puzzle pieces, we don't use the preposition "about". The "mystery" isn't the focus of the pieces. The preposition "about" is a scope. If we use the preposition "about", the scope would be the mystery, or more specifically, the whole picture of the solved mystery. But we don't have the whole picture. We're trying to put the pieces together. So maybe you can say that each piece is part of the scope, but that's a little strange. Either way, that's not what this sentence would mean if we use the preposition "about".

FROM: The logic of the preposition "from" kind of makes sense here, but let's talk about a puzzle instead of a mystery (in order) to make this easier to understand. We can use the preposition "from" when we're talking about puzzles, but not in this context.

There are two contexts that work: 1) you're talking about an individual piece itself, instead of it's relation to the whole. For example, you find a random puzzle piece on the floor that fell when you were putting the pieces away yesterday. You pick it up and say, "I think this is (a piece) from the puzzle that I was doing yesterday". You can still use the prepositions "to" and "of" in this case.

2) You have two puzzles and some of the pieces get mixed together. You have to sort them out. You say, "Ok, it looks like this piece is from puzzle A, but I think that piece is from puzzle B". In that case, you can still use the preposition "to": "It looks like this piece goes to/belongs to puzzle A". Or you can use the preposition "of": "It looks like this piece is part of puzzle A".

So the preposition "from" is possible, but it depends on the exact context and how you're talking about things. Because we're talking about a mystery, which is like a puzzle but is not a puzzle, the preposition "from" doesn't quite work, at least in this context where we're talking about pieces of a mystery.

10) Do you remember what the name **of** that song is?

OF: When talking about a song, the word "name" means "title". Every song has a name/title, which is part of the song. It's not part of the content of the song, it's part of the song as a whole. A song has a name/title, a length (duration), the content of the song (words and music), a rhythm, etc...

FROM: It's possible to use the preposition "from", but it's much less common and the meaning is different. If you say "the name from that song", it means that in the song, the singer says a name. For example, "Maria". You don't remember what the name is that's in the song, so ask, "What's the name from that song?" because the name comes from the song. The song is the origin point and the name is inside that origin point.

11) I don't like the colors **in / of** this painting.

IN: Remember that when we talk about images (for example, pictures, drawings, paintings), it's like you're looking into a window (in order) to see a scene. English looks at the content of images as being inside the image, not on the image.

OF: This is the most common answer. The painting has a size, a shape, colors, etc... So the colors are part of the painting. Of course, in this specific case, the colors are also part of the content of the painting, so we have both parts of the logic, but they both go the same direction. This is something that rarely happens.

ON: When talking about a picture (photograph), we never use the preposition "on" unless you mean that there's something physically on the material of the picture. For example, I accidentally spill milk on the picture. Because a painting is actually an image that's applied to a surface, the colors are on the painting. Or are they? In reality, the colors are on the surface that the painting was painted on top of. When we talk about the image that we see in the painting, we don't use the preposition "on" because we're not talking about the physical surface of the painting. Instead, we're talking about the colors as being inside/part of the image. So the preposition "on" doesn't work here.

12) The size **of** this shirt is too big.

OF: In this case, we're talking about the size of the shirt, which is part of it. A shirt has a color, a size (small, medium, large), a tag, a front, a back, and sleeves. These are all parts of the shirt.

IN: Remember that we use the preposition "in" when we're talking about the size of the shirt. But that's only when we're talking about the shirt itself. For example, maybe the store has one <u>shirt in large</u>, which means that the store has one shirt with the size "large". "Do you have this shirt in large?" "Does this shirt come in large?" However, in the sentence, "The size of this shirt is too big", we're not talking about the shirt (in which case "size" = "the size of the container (shirt)". Instead, we're talking about the size itself. "Large" is the <u>size of the shirt</u>. Remember that the size is part of the shirt, just like the front and the back of the shirt are parts. This is why the context is important. It depends exactly what you're talking about and what you want to say. The preposition "of" is much more logical in this case than the preposition "in".

Explain the Logic 1

Instructions: Look at each sentence and explain how the logic of each preposition works in that particular sentence. Don't look in the main book and don't look at the previous explanations that are in this book. It might be difficult to describe, but the goal here isn't to describe it perfectly. This exercise will help you more fully understand each preposition's logic by trying to put it into your own words. It will also test how well you can currently feel the logic. Explanations of each sentence are on the next page.

1) **In** learning a language, **at** what point can you consider yourself fluent?

2) We're finished **with** today's class. See you **on** Monday.

3) This is my favorite thing **in** the world! I wouldn't sell it **for** anything.

4) "I can't get the layout (that's) **on** my website **to** work!" "Leave it **to** me. I'll make it look great!"

5) Good morning class. **To** start **off**, let's look **at** the homework.

6) The police finally caught him. It was difficult because he was operating **under** an alias.

7) Sorry, I interrupted you. What were you **about to** say?

8) "Give me all (**of**) your money!" "**Over** my dead body!" (idiom)

9) I'll be there **in** a flash. (very quickly)

10) What class are you doing homework **for**?

Explanations

1) **In** learning a language, **at** what point can you consider yourself fluent?

IN: "Learning a language" is a process. Inside of that process, we can talk about something else that happens.

AT: The second part of this sentence is something that happens or can happen in the process of learning a language. In this case, we're asking a question about a specific point in that process, so we use the preposition "at": "<u>At what point</u> (in that process) can you consider yourself fluent?" In other words, "When will you be fluent?"

In this specific case, you can also look at the phrase "in learning a language" as a timeline because it takes time to learn a language. There are certain points (in time) on that timeline, and we can be <u>at</u> one of those specific points.

2) We're finished **with** today's class. See you **on** Monday.

WITH: If the class time for the day has ended, we can say that it's "finished". A class is something that you use (in order) to learn. When the time for the day ends, then you're finished "using" the class. Another way to look at it in this case is with the verb "to have". Notice that we say, "I have a class today", which means that you have to go to a particular class today. When the class time ends, you're "finished (with) having class". Of course, the basic idea of the preposition "with" is "together". You're in class, then you're not, so you and the class (or the process of having class) are not together anymore.

ON: As you know, the day of the week is the <u>active</u> day, which can also be like a special abstract platform.

3) This is my favorite thing **in** the world! I wouldn't sell it **for** anything.

IN: A world is a container. It's very common that we use the word "world" when we mean "the planet Earth". However, these two are not the same thing. If you say "in the

115

earth", it means that something is inside the earth, meaning underground. Earth is a planet, so when we talk about being on it, we say, "on (the) Earth". We don't normally say that instead of "in the world", because "in the world" doesn't mean "on a planet". It's a different context. A world is more like the totality of a large environment. We can talk about a world of dreams or a world of peace, for example. Or if you're really lost in your thoughts and don't notice your friend who's trying to get your attention, when you notice them, you can say, "Sorry, I was lost in my own little world".

FOR: This is the idea of exchanging one basis for another basis.

4) "I can't get the layout (that's) **on** my website **to** work!" "Leave it **to** me. I'll make it look great!"

ON: A website is like an abstract platform because you access it (in order) to do something. Just like we have social media platforms, which have the purpose of interacting with other people, a specific website has a specific purpose. For example, if you go to google.com, you'll find the google search engine. The purpose of this search engine is to help you find information on the internet.

TO: We know that the preposition "to" can turn a verb into an end point. Let's break this sentence into pieces: "I can't get" + "the layout" + "(that's) on my website" + "to work".

"I can't get" = What am I doing? Trying to get the layout to work. Can I do it? No.

I can't get what? = "the layout"

Which layout? = The one that's on my website

I can't get the layout (that's) on my website… = What do I want? Do I want to get the layout? No, I already have the layout that I want (maybe a drawing on paper), but I can't make the layout look the way that I want it to on the website. So, what do I want the layout <u>to</u> do? What's the end point? What's the end action that I want to happen? "Work", which in this case means "work properly", "function properly", or

116

"look the way that I want it to". So, "work" is the result that I want. "To" + "work" = "to" → work" = "to work".

"I can't get the layout (that's) on my website" + "to → work".

TO: This is an interesting case. "Leave it to me" means that I'm telling you that I'll do it and that you don't have to worry about it. In other words, I'm doing it for you. Normally, when we exchange one basis for another basis, we use the preposition "for", like I just did in the sentence, "I'm doing it for you". However, what if we say, "Leave it <u>for</u> me"? The meaning and context are completely different. This sentence means that I want you to leave something so that I can get it (purpose), or that I want you to leave something simply because I asked (basis).

So why do we use the preposition "to"? Because I'm the end point. The sentence, "Leave it to me" really means is: "Give the responsibility to me." Now we can see that I'm the receiver, which is a type of end point. The preposition "to" here is the same as it is in the sentence, "Send the letter to me". So, in this context (and with this meaning of the verb "to leave"), you can see that we're not talking about exchanging one basis for another, but it might seem that way.

5) Good morning class. **To** start **off**, let's look **at** the homework.

TO: This is another case where the meaning is "in order to", but we would probably never say "in order". We don't just drop it, we simply don't say it. However, it's clear here that we're talking about a purpose (starting the class). But we have something else that's interesting here. "To" + "start off", "..." We're using the infinitive form of the verb "to start", so really, it's one big chunk: "To start off". Ok, then what? "To start off" → "Let's look at the homework". We're actually using the preposition "to" (in order) to point to "start off", but the whole phrase "to start off" then points to the action of "look at the homework". So this is a special combination of groups four and five in the main book.

117

OFF: We can use the preposition "off" with the meaning of "starting to move away from a central point". Or, more simply in this case, just "starting". The central platform is the start of the class, which is the starting point in time when the class begins. From that point, we move forward until we reach the end of the class. In other words, we're using the start/origin point as the central platform.

More specifically, the preposition "off" in this sentence is very similar to the preposition "off" in the sentence, "I'm off to work", which is when you leave home (the central platform) and start the process of traveling to work. The only real difference is that the sentence "I'm off to work" is a process that's focused on distance (home to work = point A in space to point B in space), but when we say "To start off (the class)", the process is focused on time (start of the class to the end of the class = point A in time to point B in time). We can see that the logic of the preposition "off" is the same in both sentences, but the logic is being applied in two different ways that are similar.

AT: "The homework" is the target of your vision. In this case, it's not just about physically looking at the homework, it's about discussing the homework and seeing what the answers are. So here, the target is really all of that and not just a physical piece of paper.

6) The police finally caught him. It was difficult because he was operating **under** an alias.

UNDER: An alias a fake name that you use for some purpose. In this case, there's a criminal. Instead of using his real name, he told people his name was something else, so it was difficult for the police to find him. We use the verb "to operate" because he was running some sort of criminal organization or process, like selling drugs.

We use the preposition "under" because he can use his real name or another name. If my name is "Josh" and I operate under the alias "Tom", then everything that I do is attached to the name "Tom". It's very similar to the library categories example

118

that we saw in the book: "HISTORY" → "WWII" → "AXIS POWERS" → "GERMANY" → etc... All of the smaller/lower categories are under the larger/higher categories. Instead of "HISTORY" → "WWII", we could look under "HISTORY" → "ANCIENT GREECE", for example. So if I use the alias "Tom", then all of the different things that I do using that name goes under that name. "Tom" is like the label that identifies the source of all of the activities. Then the downward force of the preposition "under" organizes those activities into a hierarchy.

7) Sorry, I interrupted you. What were you **about to** say?

ABOUT + TO: We saw an example like this earlier and a few examples in the main book. You were speaking. I interrupted you. Before that, you were going to say something. We have a timeline:

You're speaking → you're going to say something → I interrupt you

The scope is around the point "you're going to say something" and "I interrupt you". See the preposition "about", group three in the main book for more information.

8) "Give me all (**of**) your money!" "**Over** my dead body!" (idiom)

OF: "All of you money" is 100% of your money, or at least 100% of the money that you have with you. We're talking about a part, but in this case, the part is the whole.

OVER: This idiom basically means, "You'll have to kill me first". In other words, it's a very strong way to say, "NO!" You can use this phrase in situations where no one is going to kill you, which is actually more common, but in this sentence, the person might actually kill you.

But why do we use the preposition "over" and how does it create that meaning? Simple. I want your money. You won't give it to me and tell me that I have to kill you if I want it. I kill you, take the money, walk over your dead body, and

119

leave ("Walk over" in this context means that I take a step forward so that I pass above your body and continue walking forward after I reach the other side of your body). Of course, if someone kills someone, they can go in the opposite direction and not walk over the body, but it's an idiom. The meaning doesn't have to be literal.

But there's a little more here than just going to the other side of a dead body. When someone says, "Over my dead body!", they're really saying that they're not just going to do what you want, in this case, give you money. They're making themselves the obstacle that you have to abstractly reach the other side of if you want to take the money. Imagine that the money is behind that person and the person is a fence. If you want the money, you have to go over the fence. Except in this case, the fence is going to try to stop you from reaching the other side, so you have to "kill" the fence. Then there's no obstacle and you can take the money.

9) I'll be there **in** a flash. (very quickly)

IN: This one might seem strange, but it's very simple. The word "flash" means "very quickly". It has several meanings, but think of lightning from the sky. Light travels very quickly. When lightning comes out of the sky and hits the ground, it moves extremely quickly. We often just call this "lightning", but an individual bolt (piece) of lightning is also called a flash of lightning.

Ok, that's what the word "flash" means, but why do we use the preposition "in"? What if I say, "I'll be there in a minute" or "I'll be there in a two days"? Yes, it's the same as those examples. "In a flash" means "in a very short amount of time". Obviously, you can't move at the speed of light, so it's an exaggeration, but the purpose of saying this is to tell the person that you're coming immediately and you'll be there as fast as you can. If you're really far away, like in another state, then this phrase loses meaning because you simply can't get there quickly.

10) What class are you doing homework **for**?

FOR: I intentionally made this a question so that the preposition "for" is at the end of the sentence. The statement version or answer would be, "I'm doing homework for math class", for example. This can be both a purpose and a basis. If the homework is for math class, then the purpose of the homework is to learn math and eventually to pass the class. But we can also say that "math class" is the basis. If the homework comes from math class, then the homework is based on the subject of math. If it comes from history class, then it's based on the subject of history.

Prepositions in Real Contexts: Fill-in-the-Blanks

Instructions: There are ten short articles/stories. Fill in all of the blank spaces. There might be more than one correct answer, but because these are specific contexts, we only want prepositions that work in each specific context.

IMPORTANT NOTE: These are normal stories/articles, so there are other prepositions like "after", "through", "during", etc... Because we're only focusing on the logic of seventeen prepositions, the other prepositions are still in the text and you don't have to worry about them.

1) Tom's Horrible Day

Last week, Tom woke __ everyday __ six __ the morning. He made a cup __ coffee __ sugar, ate breakfast, spoke __ his wife a little, and then left __ work __ seven. This morning, he forgot his keys and had __ go back __ __ get them. When he tried __ start the car, it didn't start. "Great!" He said as he got __ __ the car. Now he had __ take the bus.

He grabbed some things __ the car and brought them __ him __ the bus stop. As he waited, he started thinking. He hated his job and was thinking __ quitting. He felt like he was just existing and not making any impact __ the world. He wanted __ find a new job that he liked, but he didn't know what kind __ job that might be.

The bus arrived and it looked very crowded. He got __ , but couldn't find an empty seat. He put his bag __ the floor and continued __ think __ his job. He thought he was wasting his life. He wanted __ get a promotion. Maybe that would help. No, he wanted something different, something more. He knew life had more __ offer.

The bus arrived __ his stop. He looked __ and noticed that his bag was gone! He got __ the bus and wondered if this day could get any worse. A tall, poor, angry man walked __ __ him and asked him __ money. Tom remembered that his wallet was __ his bag. Tom told the man that he didn't have any money. The man didn't believe him and punched him __ the face. Tom fell __ the ground and started crying. He couldn't even call his wife __ pick him __ because his phone was __ the bag, too. This was the worst day __ his life!

Someone heard him crying and asked if he needed help. He looked __ and saw a woman. He didn't know her. Why would a complete stranger help him? Tom told her everything. The kind woman gave him twenty dollars and allowed him __ use her phone. __ that moment, Tom realized what he wanted __ do __ life: help people less fortunate than himself. He called his wife and excitedly told her the good news.

2) The Universe

The universe is all __ space and time and their contents, including planets, stars, galaxies, and all other forms __ matter and energy. While the spatial size __ the entire Universe is still unknown, it is possible __ measure the observable universe.

The earliest scientific models __ the Universe were developed __ ancient Greek and Indian philosophers and were geocentric, placing Earth __ the center __ the Universe. __ the centuries, more precise astronomical observations led Nicolas Copernicus __ develop the heliocentric model __ the Sun __ the center __ the Solar System. __ developing the law __ universal gravitation, Sir Isaac Newton built __ Copernicus' work.

Further observational improvements led __ the realization that our Sun is one __ hundreds __ billions __ stars __ a galaxy we call the Milky Way, which is one __ at least hundreds __ billions __ galaxies __ the Universe. Many __ the stars __ our galaxy have planets. (1)

124

3) Buying a New Computer

Today's a busy day. Many people are walking __ and __ the street outside __ Lena's store. One __ them, a tall man (who's) wearing a hat, enters the store.

"Hello! How are you?" Lena asks.

"Good. And you?"

"I'm great. What can I help you __?"

"I'm looking __ a new computer."

"Ok. Do you know what kind?"

"Not really. I need it __ run quickly. It's __ my son."

"Does he play video games?"

"Yes."

"Are they high performance?"

"I think so."

"Well," Lena says. She walks __ __ one __ the computers (that are) __ display. "We have this new model (that is) __ Super Computers."

"No. My son specifically asked __ a computer that isn't made __ Super Computers. He hates them."

"Ok, we have lots __ other computers." Lena walks __ a computer that's __ the middle __ the store. "This one just came __ last month. It has a lot __ power."

"How much is it?"

"$1,200."

"Wow! That's really expensive. I don't want __ pay __ $1,000. Do you have one that's cheaper?"

Lena points __ another computer. "I think that one would work well. It's only $800. Anything cheaper than that probably won't work well __ video games."

"I'll take it."

After the man pays __ the computer, he takes the computer and walks __ __ the store.

4) The Black Cat

Lena's walking home. It's five __ the evening and she's very tired after a long day __ work. Suddenly, Lena sees a black cat __ front __ her! She's afraid because a black cat means bad luck. She tries __ cross the street, but the black cat stops her.

"Where are you going?" The black cat asks.
"I'm going __ the other side __ the street," Lena says.
"Why?"
"Because you're a black cat and everyone knows that black cats are bad luck."
"That's not true! I'm just a cat."
"A talking cat."
"Yes, I'm a talking cat. I think that means (that) I'm lucky."
"I think that means (that) I'm __ __ my mind. But how do I know (that) you're telling the truth?"
"Because black cats are very honest. __ the way, do you have any food __ you?"
"No, but I can give you some if you come __ me __ my house."
"You're going __ take a talking cat home __ you?"
"Sure. You can tell me __ how you can talk __ dinner. Anyway, I can't just leave you __ __ the cold."
"Yay! Let's go!"

5) World War I

   World War I (often abbreviated as WWI or WW1), also known as the First World War or the Great War, was a global war originating __ Europe that lasted __ 28 July 1914 __ 11 November 1918. Described __ the time as the "War __ End All Wars", more than 70 million military personnel, including 60 million Europeans, were mobilized __ one __ the largest wars __ history. __ nine million combatants and seven million civilians died as a result __ the war (including the victims __ a number __ genocides). It was one __ the deadliest conflicts __ history and led __ major political change, including the Revolutions __ 1917–

126

1923 __ many __ the nations involved. Unresolved rivalries __ the end __ the conflict contributed __ the start __ the Second World War twenty-one years later.

The war drew __ all the world's great economic powers, assembled __ two opposing alliances: the Allies (based __ the Triple Entente __ the Russian Empire, the French Third Republic, and the United Kingdom) versus the Central Powers __ Germany and Austria-Hungary. Although Italy was a member __ the Triple Alliance alongside Germany and Austria-Hungary, it did not join the Central Powers. (2)

6) <u>The Strange House</u>

Two days ago, a friend and I were walking __ night. We heard a strange sound coming __ an old house. I've heard a lot __ strange sounds __ my life, but this was particularly strange. I can't describe it. My friend said that we shouldn't go __, but I wanted __ because it seemed empty. I had __ find __ if something was inside or not.

We cautiously entered the house. The sound was louder inside. __ some reason, it smelled like tea. Suddenly, we saw a blue light coming __ a room __ the right. My friend was nervous. He said we should leave, but I told him that there had __ be a logical explanation and that we would be fine.

__ be honest, part __ me wanted __ leave. I wasn't sure if my friend was going __ leave me there. I looked behind me and he was still there. Good. I slowly moved closer __ the door. The sound stopped. I stopped. Even my heart seemed __ stop. The door started __ open. I couldn't move. I had __ move! The door opened.

127

7) The Broken Heart

Today, Alex is reading __ a tall, green tree. He's reading his favorite book, which has all __ his favorite stories __ it. The first story is __ a man who has a horrible day. The second story is __ a black cat. The third story is __ a strange house.

As Alex reads, something hits him __ the head. He looks __ and sees a small, white heart. It's broken. He picks it __ and looks __ __ find whose heart it is. There's no one __. It's quiet. Alex goes home and brings the heart __ him. That night, he fixes the heart.

The next day, he comes back __ the same place __ the broken heart. Someone is __ the tree. It's a mean, old man __ a dog.
"Is this your heart?" Alex asks.
"No!" the old man says. "Go away!"

So, Alex goes away and comes back later that day. A different person is __ the tree. It's a young child.
"Is this your heart?" Alex asks.
"No." The child says.

Alex leaves again and comes back __ the evening. He sees someone looking __ the tree __ something. It's a beautiful, young woman.
"Is this your heart?" Alex asks.
"My heart! You stole it!"
"No. It hit me yesterday when I was reading. I came back here __ return it."
"Please give it __ me."
Alex gives her the heart.
"Oh, I thought it was broken. Did you fix it?"
"Yes," Alex says.

The beautiful, young woman becomes very happy and falls __ love __ Alex.

128

8) <u>Language Learning</u>

Language learning is a big and complicated task __ many different parts. A language isn't just one thing; it's a group __ skills: speaking, listening, writing, and reading, as well as pronunciation. __ course, vocabulary and grammar are also big parts __ learning a language. However, a grammar-based approach __ language learning will usually fail. Grammar can be useful, but trying __ learn a language through grammar is like trying __ learn how __ ride a bike __ reading a maintenance manual or studying physics. So where should you start?

There are different opinions __ this topic. __ some people's opinion (__ example, Steve Kaufmann (check __ his YouTube channel)), you should start __ focusing __ listening and reading a lot. Other people, like Benny Lewis (also check __ his YouTube channel), say the exact opposite: "Speak __ day one!" Which one is better __ learning a new language? It depends __ you and how you prefer __ learn.

It's true that we all learn a little differently. The traditional idea is that some people are "auditory" learners (listening-based), others are "visual" learners (sight-based), and others are "kinesthetic" learners (based __ doing/physical use). These are partially true, but they don't matter because language learning is a set __ four __ five skills.

__ example, the skill __ listening is, __ course, listening-based. If you're a "visual learner", maybe you see the words __ your head while you listen, and that's fine, but the point is that the only way __ get really good __ listening __ a foreign language and understanding it is __ listen a lot. __ course, knowing the language's pronunciation can help a lot, too, but even if you know all __ the pronunciation rules, if you never actually listen __ the language, you'll never be able __ understand what you hear, especially when people speak quickly.

Answers and Explanations

1) <u>Tom's Horrible Day</u>

Last week, Tom woke **up** everyday **at** six **in** the morning.

UP: It's possible to simply say, "Tome woke", so we don't really need the preposition "up", but "woke up" is so common that it sounds a little better. When you're sleeping, you're conscious awareness is inactive. It's like you're inside your mind under the surface of "awake". When you wake up, your conscious awareness becomes active and you're above the surface. So the preposition "up" is connecting to the logic of the preposition "on" because if you're awake, it's very similar to a light that's turned on. It's like your conscious awareness is now "on".

AT: This is a specific hour of the day and a specific point in time.

IN: The morning, afternoon, and evening are all periods of time during the day. They seem small, but compared to the 24 hours of one day, they're actually large periods of time, so we use the preposition "in" because they're containers. Imagine that the parts of the day are divided and put into boxes.

Of course, the one exception to this is "at night". The reason that we say "at night" is probably because the night is the time that most people sleep. While we're sleeping, it's like one point in time, because you go to sleep and then it's morning. It's like a single specific moment passes because we're not consciously aware that time is passing.

Also, if "in the morning" is a container, you can do different things, which is like putting things into the container. But at night, you don't do anything except sleep, so there's no reason to make it a container that you would put different things into.

He made a cup **of** coffee **with** sugar, ate breakfast, spoke **with** his wife a little, and then left **for** work **at** seven.

131

OF: "A cup" is a particular amount of coffee, so it can be a part. How much coffee compared to the total amount? One cup. Of course, the coffee is also the content that's inside the cup.

WITH: He put the coffee and sugar <u>together</u>, so now his coffee <u>has</u> sugar in it.

WITH: He and his wife spoke about one or more topics together.

FOR: "Work" is the destination, which is an end point. But we're using the preposition "for" and not the preposition "to". Because we can use both the preposition "for" and the phrase "in order to" when we want to talk about a purpose, sometimes these two are interchangeable (they overlap). So, we can also say, "left in order to go to work". Either way, the reason (purpose) that he left is to go to work. Notice that "work" is the destination, but we can't just use the preposition "to" without the meaning of "(in order) to". This is because "work" isn't just a destination in this context. He has to work so that he can make money, which is a purpose, so going to that destination has a particular purpose.

AT: This is a specific hour of the day and a specific point in time.

This morning, he forgot his keys and had **to** go back **in to** get them.

TO: This is the structure "have to do", which we talked about a lot in the main book.

IN: This is short for "inside (the house)". A house is a building, which is like a big container.

TO: This is "in order to". The only way he can get the keys (ability) is to go back into the house. The purpose of going back into the house is to get his keys. Of course, the purpose of all of that is so that he can drive his car, which is implied by the context.

When he tried **to** start the car, it didn't start. "Great!" He said as he got **out of** the car. Now he had **to** take the bus.

132

TO: "Try to do" is like "want to do", "need to do", "have to do", etc... He makes an attempt (another word for "try") and that attempt/try points to the action of starting the car. The idea of the verb "to try" is to test if something works or not. We then point that test to the action/verb (in order) to specify what action that we're testing.

Note that just like we have "I want to go" and "I want ice cream", we only need the preposition "to" when we point to an action/verb and not a thing: "I tried to go" and "I tried ice cream".

OUT: He was in(side) the car, which is like a container, and now he's not.

OF: In this case, we have to use the preposition "of". There are some people who break this rule, but it sounds very informal. The reason that we need it here is because "got out the car" means that he brought the car out of the garage; the car was stuck somewhere and got it unstuck; or he took a toy car out of some container (a box, his pocket, etc...). It's also more common to say, "got the car out" in those cases. Because we have these other meanings when we don't use the preposition "of", the preposition "of" in "got out of the car" helps to keep the meaning clear.

But how does the logic work here? He was inside the car. that's part of the car. A car has an inside and an outside, which by extension includes everything that is located outside of the car. So he moved from the inside part to the outside part.

Noe that it's also possible to say, "get out from the car", but it's less common.

TO: This is the structure "have to do", which we talked about a lot in the main book.

He grabbed some things **from/in** the car and brought them **with** him **to** the bus stop.

FROM: The things that he grabbed were in the car and he took them out of the car, so it's also possible in this case to say, "He grabbed some things out of the car". We can

133

also use the preposition "from" in this case because the inside of the car is the origin point from which he grabs the things. Notice that the preposition "from" replaces the preposition "out" in this case, but we saw that when we say, "He got out of the car", the preposition "from" replaces the preposition "of". The difference here is because in one case he's removing himself from the car, but in the other case he's removing something else from the car.

IN: We can also use the preposition "in" here. The things that he grabs are in the car, which is a container. You can also use "from in(side) the car". Even if we only use the preposition "in" and not the preposition "from", the preposition "from" is implied, but we need either "in" or "from". In other words, we can't just say "He grabbed some things the car".

WITH: After he grabs the things, he and those things are <u>together</u>, so he <u>has</u> them.

TO: "The bus stop" is the destination/end point.

As he waited, he started thinking. He hated his job and was thinking **about/of** quitting. He felt like he was just existing and not making any impact **on/in** the world. He wanted **to** find a new job that he liked, but he didn't know what kind **of** job that might be.

ABOUT: We saw a sentence in the main book: "Think about trees". This is the same, except Tom's thinking about a verb/action. When you think about something, you put your attention and focus onto it, which excludes all other things that you could think about instead. This creates the "scope" of your thought.

OF: We can also use the preposition "of" here. Remember that sometimes these two prepositions overlap and sometimes they just touch. Other times, they're completely separate. It just depends on the context and what you want to say. In the main book (preposition "of", group two), we saw that when we have the structure "verb" of "verbing", the second verb is the content of the first verb. What's the content of his thoughts? The action of quitting.

ON: When we use the word "impact", we can often use both the preposition "on" and the preposition "in", but it depends on the specific context. In this case, we can use both. The preposition "on" works because the basic meaning of the word "impact" is when one surface hits another surface. In this sentence, which is more abstract, we extend that basic meaning. Making an impact on/in the world means to make a difference. In other words, he wants to have a positive effect that will help people. If you just work a job that doesn't actually help people – or worse, a job that hurts people – then you're not making an impact (or you're making a negative impact). By default, an "impact" is usually a positive effect, but we can also talk about a "negative impact". For example, if a company pollutes the environment.

IN: The preposition "in" works because he wants to have a positive effect, and that positive effect happens somewhere in the world. We can also say that he's in the world while he's trying to make the impact.

TO: This is the structure "want to do", which we talked about a lot in the main book.

OF: We use the preposition "of" after the words "kind", "type", and "sort" when these words mean a version of something. For example: "What kind of fruit do you like?" → "I like bananas and apples." Apples and bananas are specific fruits, and "fruit" is the category word. "Apple" and "banana" are the content that replace the word "fruit". So this is a special case. We're still using the "content" part of the logic of the preposition "of", but we're not saying that the thing after the preposition "of" is the content of the thing before the preposition "of". For example, "This table is made of wood" → "wood" is the content of the table. Instead, what we're doing when we use "kind of" is we're saying that there's a more specific version than the category word. For example, "fruit" is the category word for "apple". What kind of fruit? Apple. "Apple" is the content of "fruit".

135

The bus arrived and it looked very crowded. He got **on**, but couldn't find an empty seat. He put his bag **on** the floor and continued **to** think **about** his job.

ON: A bus is a transportation platform.

ON: The floor is a surface.

TO: "Continue" + "to" + "think". This is like "want to think", "need to think", etc... except he's simply continuing what he was already doing.

ABOUT: His job is the scope of his thoughts.

He thought he was wasting his life. He wanted **to** get a promotion. Maybe that would help. No, he wanted something different, something more. He knew life had more **to** offer.

TO: "Want" + 'to" + "get" (meaning: receive).

TO: Here we see "have to" with the word "more" in between. First note that this is not "have to do something", meaning an obligation. That would be: "Life had to offer more". Instead, we're using the basic meaning of the verb "to have": "Life had…" We add the word "more": "Life had more..." More what? "More to offer". This is like saying, "I have something to offer you", which means that I have something and I want to offer it to you.

So, life can have more experiences, for example, which is a noun. But we're using a verb: "to offer". Just like with "I want ice cream" and "I want to go", we have the same thing, expect we're adding the word "more": "Life has more experiences" and "Life has more to offer". We still need the preposition "to" (in order) to point to the action/verb.

The bus arrived **at** his stop. He looked **down** and noticed that his bag was gone! He got **off** the bus and wondered if this day could get any worse.

AT: A "bus stop" is a specific location where buses stop so that people can get on.

DOWN: He's standing and his back was on the floor, so he looks downwards (direction).

136

OFF: Because a bus is a transportation platform, when you exit the bus, you get off of that platform.

A tall, poor, angry man walked **up/over to** him and asked him **for** money. Tom remembered that his wallet was **in** his bag.

UP: Tom's the central platform because we're talking about things from his perspective and the man is getting closer to him.

OVER: The man goes from where he was to another point. The distance doesn't have to be long, but it often is. It's similar to saying, "Come over here" when the person who you're talking to is just on the other side of the room. And that's another good point: a "long distance" can be relative. If someone is on the other side of a room, they're not very far away, but if we just focus on the size of the room and nothing else, then the opposite side of the room is "far". It's the opposite side of that space. The preposition "over" in cases like this usually add a little emphasis. Tom's at a particular point. When we say, "The man walked over to him", it sounds like the man wasn't close to Tom before. Maybe he was on the other side of the street or he was sitting on a chair that was 15 feet away (4.5 meters).

TO: Tom is the end point, meaning that his specific location is the man's destination.

FOR: The purpose of the question ("ask") is to receive money.

IN: A bag is a container.

Tom told the man that he didn't have any money. The man didn't believe him and punched him **in** the face. Tom fell **to/on** the ground and started crying.

IN: Remember that when we're talking about the body, if something hits you, but the hit (impact) doesn't have a lot of force, we use the preposition "on" because two surfaces are touching. But if it's more forceful, we use the preposition "in" (in order) to show that extra force.

TO: If you fall, the ground can be an end point. You're standing and then you fall downwards, so you're moving closer to the ground until you land on it.

ON: The ground is a surface.

He couldn't even call his wife **to** pick him **up** because his phone was **in** the bag, too. This was the worst day **of/in** his life!

TO: This is short for (in order) to, but this is another case where the "in order" sounds a little strange if we actually say it. However, it's clear that the purpose of calling his wife is so that he doesn't have to walk home, which also gives him the ability to get home faster.

UP: "Pick someone up" means that you are going to drive to a location where someone is waiting for you and take them to another location. The preposition "up" connects to the logic of the preposition "on", but if you're driving a car, truck, or other personal vehicle, the preposition we use is the preposition "in". We can use "pick someone up" if we're talking about both a bus and a car. With a bus, it makes sense: a bus is a large vehicle that transports many people, so it's a transportation platform that you get on, so we can connect to that idea with the preposition "up", but that's not actually what's happening here. With a car, it might seem like it doesn't make sense, but think about it. You get in(to) a car. We don't say that the bus is going to pick you on and we don't say that a car is going to pick you in, so the specific preposition doesn't matter here. If I use my arms to physically pick you up and carry you somewhere, I'm transporting you to that location. It's the same with a bus and a car. Your feet aren't on the ground anymore because something is "carrying" you to a new location. So you're up and off of the ground.

This is why we use the verb "to pick" in this phrasal verb. Imagine a giant hand that comes out of the sky and grabs your body. This is like if you reach down to the ground and pick something up. The reason that you pick it up is so that you can move it to another location.

IN: A bag is a container.

138

OF: As you live, minutes pass, days pass, years pass, etc... We're talking about days in this case. He's an adult, so he's lived through many days, but we're saying that out of all of the days that he's been alive, this is the worse one. So "day" is part of "life", but we're also saying that "day" is part of the total number of days in his life until now.

IN: The preposition "in" in this context is not as common, but it works. Your life is a period of time and things happen inside that period. In this case, we're saying that the day is the worst day he's experienced in his life.

Someone heard him crying and asked if he needed help. He looked **up/around/over** and saw a woman.

UP: Tom's on the ground. The person is standing, so he has to look upward. This is probably the most common answer in this context.

AROUND: We can also use the preposition "around". If he hears the voice near him, but not really close (next to) him, he might look around to find the person who's talking. "Around" in this case can mean "in a circle" (group one), "in a semi-circle" (group two), or "in the general area of a specific point" (he's the specific point; group three).

OVER: Lastly, we can also use the preposition "over". This is like the preposition "around" because the voice isn't really close to him, but the preposition "over" specifically means "to the side" in this context. He hears the voice either to the left or to the right of where he is.

He didn't know her. Why would a complete stranger help him? Tom told her everything. The kind woman gave him twenty dollars and allowed him **to** use her phone. **At/In** that moment, Tom realized what he wanted **to** do **in** life: help people less fortunate than himself. He called his wife and excitedly told her the good news.

TO: This is the "allow to do" structure. Here, we have the word "him" between "allow" and "to". This is mostly just

139

grammar structure and it tells us exactly who she allowed. It doesn't change the "allow" + "to" + "do" idea.

AT: We're talking about the specific moment in time when Tom receives twenty dollars and can use her phone.

IN: Remember that we can often go "into" the preposition "at" when talking about time and space, but it depends on the specific context. Just like you can be inside a store when you're at that store, we can talk about being inside a moment when you're at that moment. Be careful. Words like "that", "this", and "the" before words like "moment" can sometimes affect the preposition.

TO: This is "want to do".

IN: Again, we see the preposition "in" with the word "life". Instead of talking about the days of his life, we're talking about what he wants to do as a job during his life.

2) The Universe

The universe is all **of** space and time and their contents, including planets, stars, galaxies, and all other forms **of** matter and energy. While the spatial size **of** the entire Universe is still unknown, it is possible **to** measure the observable universe.

OF: This is "all of X". "All" means "all parts", so we're saying that the universe is "all parts of space and all parts of time and all parts of their contents". This might seem really abstract and confusing, but that's because we're talking about "all of" something, in this case, all of existence.

OF: "Matter" and "energy" are the content of the forms. We can also say that the form is part of the matter and the energy because a form is only part of something. For example, matter also has density.

OF: Here we see another example with the word "size" and the preposition "of". The universe has a size, which is only one part or characteristic.

TO: "It is possible" + "to" + "do". Again, we see the preposition "to" pointing to an action and connecting it to

140

something before it. In this case, we're talking about a possibility. That possibility point to the action of measuring.

The earliest scientific models **of** the Universe were developed **by** ancient Greek and Indian philosophers and were geocentric, placing Earth **at** the center **of** the universe.

OF: The universe is the content of the models. What kind of models? Models of trees? Models of thinking? No, models of the universe.

BY: This is passive voice: "were developed by". They are the abstract source through which the models were created.

AT: The center of the universe is a specific point, just like the center of a room or the center of a city.

OF: The universe can also have a center. Size, center, edge, colors, etc… are all possible parts or characteristics.

Over the centuries, more precise astronomical observations led Nicolas Copernicus **to** develop the heliocentric model **with** the sun **at** the center **of** the solar system.

OVER: Many centuries passed starting from the time of ancient Greece and India until the time when Nicolas Copernicus lived. We can use the preposition "over" (in order) to talk about the "more precise astronomical observations" that developed during those centuries. The preposition "over" also gives us a little extra feeling of traveling all the way from point A in time to point B in time.

TO: We often use the preposition "to" after the verb "to lead" (past tense: "led"). We can talk about one thing leading to another thing. For example, "The invention of the internet led to the creation of Google". The first thing caused the second thing, or at least the existence of the first thing allowed the second thing to happen, so in this case we can say that the first thing points to the second thing, because it's the result of the first thing.

In the sentence, it says, "more precise astronomical observations **led** Nicolas Copernicus **to** develop..." There's something different about this example. The name "Nicolas

141

Copernicus" is between the words "led" and "to". This is because he's doing the action ("develop"). So we're saying that one thing led a person to do something. The idea is the same, but we're adding a person between the two things. So the logic is "lead" + "to" + "something" or "lead" + "someone" + "to" + "do something".

WITH: In the heliocentric model, the sun is at the center of the solar system. So part of this model is the location of the sun. If the sun isn't at the center, it's not the heliocentric model. We need the sun at the center. With the sun at the center, we have the model. In other words, the heliocentric model has the sun at the center.

AT: This is the same as "at the center of the universe". Instead of talking about the center of the universe, we're talking about the center of the solar system.

OF: Instead of talking about the center of the universe, we're talking about the center of the solar system.

In developing the law **of** universal gravitation, Sir Isaac Newton built **on** Copernicus' work.

IN: Notice "in" + "developing", which is a process. In this process (action 1), Newton built on... (action 2).

OF: What's the content of the law? Universal gravitation.

ON: Copernicus worked in this field of study. Later, Isaac Newton used that work as a foundation (a basis) and built on top of it. Not physically, of course. We're talking about building ideas. But the idea is the same as building a house. You need a solid foundation (base layer), and then you can build the house on top of that foundation.

Further observational improvements led **to** the realization that our sun is one **of** hundreds **of** billions **of** stars **in** a galaxy we call the Milky Way, which is one **of** at least hundreds **of** billions **of** galaxies **in** the universe. Many **of** the stars **in** our galaxy have planets.

TO: Here we see "led to" again. This is the same as the previous explanation.

OF: "One" is a part of "hundreds".

OF: Here we can say that "hundreds" is part of "billions" (How many billions? One billion? Two billion? No, hundreds.) We can also say that "billions" is the content of "hundreds". (Hundreds of what? Cars? Cats? No, billions.

OF: The number (100,000,000,000+) is the total number of stars. When we're talking about the number of something, the thing is the content of the number and the number is part of the thing. It depends on how you look at it. If there's one star, then that's a part. A star has a gravity, heat, maybe planets that orbit around it, etc… The number might not seem like a part, but it can be. If we say there are ten stars, then that number is a characteristic of the group of stars. We can also say that each star is part of the group of stars. Obviously the star is the content. One what? Ten what? A billion what? Stars. Not apples or cars, for example.

IN: A solar system <u>contains</u> a star and planets, so it's a container, especially because it's so large. That container is inside a bigger container that's called a galaxy, which of course is in the biggest container: the universe.

OF: Same as before.

OF: Same as before.

OF: Same as before.

IN: The universe is a container.

OF: "Many" isn't a specific number, but it works the same as the previous answers.

IN: A galaxy is a container.

3) <u>Buying a New Computer</u>

Today's a busy day. Many people are walking **up** and **down** the street outside **of** Lena's store. One **of** them, a tall man (who's) wearing a hat, enters the store.
"Hello! How are you?" Lena asks.
"Good. And you?"

UP and DOWN: These two prepositions can be used together in the structure "(verb) up and down (noun)". We use this when we're talking about moving along the length of something. The meaning in many cases is "back and forth", which means you go from one point to another, then back and repeat the cycle. Some examples: "He swam up and down the river", "Apply the paint up and down the wall", and "He paced up and down the hall". However, in the sentence, "People are walking up and down the street", we're not saying that each person is walking one way, then turning around and walking back, and then repeating that cycle. The meaning here is that some people are going one direction and some people are going the other direction. If you sit and watch it, it looks like "back and forth", but the people change.

The prepositions "up" and "down" work in these cases for different reasons. It depends on the context. If we're talking about painting a wall, the "up and down" is literal: an upward direction and a downward direction. But when we're talking about walking up and down a street, this is simply an extension of the ideas in the sentences: "I'm walking up the street" and "I'm walking down the street". We've talked about these sentences in the main book. If we sit and watch people who are walking along the street and some are going direction while others are going the other direction, then we can say, "People are walking up and down the street". This is because some are walking "up" the street and others are walking "down" the street. So, we can combine the "back and forth" idea with the "up the street" and "down the street" ideas (in order) to describe this scene.

OF: The preposition "of" is optional here. The store has an inside and an outside, which are parts.

OF: "One of them" = "one of the people who are walking up and down the street". Obviously, "one" is a part of the total, which we don't know, but it doesn't matter.

"I'm great. What can I help you **with**?"
"I'm looking **for** a new computer."

144

"Ok. Do you know what kind?"

"Not really. I need it **to** run quickly. It's **for** my son."

"Does he play video games?"

"Yes."

"Are they high performance?"

"I think so."

WITH: The man wants help. Help with what? We use the preposition "with" because the help and the thing that you want help with go together. In this case, he wants help with finding and buying a new computer.

FOR: The preposition "for" is often used with the verb "to look". "Look for" means "search for", but the specific context is important because sometimes one sounds better than the other. The reason that we use the preposition "for" is because you have a purpose, which is to find something. Or we can say that that thing is the basis (cause) of your search. So we can apply both parts of the logic in this case.

TO: This is the structure "need to do".

FOR: The purpose of buying the computer is so that he can give it to his son.

"Well," Lena says. She walks **over to** one **of** the computers (that are) **on** display. "We have this new model (that is) **by/from** Super Computers."

OVER: Lena is inside the store. If we say, "She walks over to" something that's inside the store, this is the same as "The man walked over to Tom". So we know that the computer that she walks over to isn't close to her before she starts walking. It might be in the middle of the store or on the other side of the store. The preposition "over" in this case is optional, but it's very common and natural.

TO: The destination is one of the computers.

OF: There's more than one computer, so the one that she's walking to is a part of the total number.

ON: We talked about this a little bit in the main book in the explanation for the sentence, "There's a sign (that's hanging) in the window". Remember that we use the preposition "on"

145

here because a display is like a special platform that has the purpose of making something visible so that people will see it.

BY: "Super Computers" is the name of the company that makes this computer. If it's a new model that is by that company, it means that that company made (created) it. They're the source. This is like the sentence, "This book was written by my father".

FROM: We can also use the preposition "from". The computer comes from the company Super Computers. That company is the origin point.

In this context, we see that the prepositions "by" and "from" overlap, which makes a lot of sense because "by" in this case is about a cause/source and the preposition "from" is about an origin point. It's clear that these two ideas are very closely related, but remember, the context is important and they're not always interchangeable.

"No. My son specifically asked **for** a computer that isn't made **by** Super Computers. He hates them."

FOR: The purpose of the question ("ask") is to receive a computer, but one that isn't made by Super Computers.

BY: We saw this explanation in the previous group of explanations.

"Ok, we have lots **of** other computers." Lena walks **to** a computer that's **in** the middle **of** the store. "This one just came **in/out** last month. It has a lot **of** power."

OF: "Computers" is the content of "lots". Lots of what? Computers. This can also be a part. For example, "We have twenty other computers". In the group of computers, there are twenty, so each computer is one part of the group. This is more about "content" than "parts", but they both work here.

TO: The computer that's in the middle of the store is the destination.

IN: The words "middle" and "center" are very similar. "Middle" comes from Germanic languages and "center" comes from Latin languages. They aren't always interchangeable, but

146

they usually mean the same thing. Both "center" and "middle" are a specific point that's between two other points (start and end, this side and that side, etc…) That point is inside the time or space of the other two points, and it's exactly or almost exactly half-way between them, so we use the preposition "in".

OF: The middle of the store is part of the store, just like the front, the back, the inside, and the outside.

IN: When a product arrives at the location of a business that will sell it, we can say that the product "comes in". We're simply saying that it arrived at the store or, more literally, that it entered the store so that the store can sell it.

OUT: We can also use the preposition "out" in this context, but the meaning is different. Instead of talking about the product arriving at the store, we're talking about the company releasing the product to the public. This is exactly like a sentence that we saw in the main book: "Is his new book out yet?". In this case, we're talking about a new computer model. It was created (it came into existence from non-existence), and it was released to the public so that people can buy it (from not released to released; outward direction from only inside the company to the public).

OF: "Power" is the content of "a lot". Note that "lots of" and "a lot of" are the same. When we use either of those, we're talking about the content, but sometimes it might also be a "part". "Power" in this context is uncountable because we're talking about the amount of power that the computer has. We can't say, "This computer has twenty powers".

"How much is it?"
"$1,200."
"Wow! That's really expensive. I don't want **to** pay **over** $1,000. Do you have one that's cheaper?"
Lena points **to** another computer. "I think that one would work well. It's only $800. Anything cheaper than that probably won't work well **with/for** video games."

TO: This is the structure "want to do".

147

OVER: This means "more than". $1000 is the obstacle (like a fence) and you don't want to go to the other side of it.

TO: The verb "to point" naturally uses the preposition "to" because whatever you point to is the end point where you want someone to look. This use of the preposition "to" includes the idea of a direction. In this case, you can also say, "point at". These aren't always interchangeable, but "another computer" can be a simple end point or a target. Remember that a target is really a specific type of end point that the preposition "at" uses (just like a purpose is a special type of end point that the preposition "for" uses). For that reason, the prepositions "to" and "at" can be confusing. This is an example where they overlap, but remember that it always depends on the context and what exactly you want to say in that context.

WITH: If you try to play video games on a computer, then it's like you're bringing the computer and the game together. More specifically, we're talking about the ability of the hardware combined with high performance video games. Put those together, and it won't work well.

FOR: This is a purpose: "for the purpose of playing video games".

"I'll take it."
After the man pays **for** the computer, he takes the computer and walks **out** **of** the store.

FOR: We use the preposition "for" because he's exchanging one basis for another basis. He's also paying for the purpose of getting the computer.

OUT: This is an outward direction from the inside of the store to the outside of the store.

OF: We talked about "out of" in the first story. Remember that the inside of something and the outside of something are parts.

4) <u>The Black Cat</u>

Lena's walking home. It's five **in** the evening and she's very tired after a long day **at/of** work. Suddenly, Lena sees a black cat **in** front **of** her! She's afraid because a black cat means bad luck. She tries **to** cross the street, but the black cat stops her.

IN: The evening is a large period (container) of time during the day.

AT: Where she works is a specific location.

OF: We can also use the preposition "of" in this case. The prepositions "of" and "at" don't usually touch or overlap, but in this context they touch. The preposition "of" works here because "work" is the content of her long day that made her tired. In other words, her day was full of nothing or almost nothing but working, so we can say that that's the content of her day.

IN: Why do we say "in front"? There's a space directly to the front of a person or a thing. That space is like a container.

OF: There's space all around her, but we're talking specifically about the space that is related to her front. This space that's in front of her isn't part of her body, but it is part of the space that's around her.

TO: This is the structure "try to do".

"Where are you going?" The black cat asks.
"I'm going **to** the other side **of** the street," Lena says.
"Why?"
"Because you're a black cat and everyone knows that black cats are bad luck."
"That's not true! I'm just a cat."
"A talking cat."

TO: The other side of the street is her destination.

OF: A street has two sides. Each side is part of the street. Of course, a sidewalk isn't part of the street, but a sidewalk is part of the area that we call "side of the street", so it still works.

"Yes, I'm a talking cat. I think that means (that) I'm lucky."

149

"I think that means (that) I'm **out of** my mind. But how do I know (that) you're telling the truth?"

"Because black cats are very honest. **By** the way, do you have any food **with/on** you?"

OUT AND OF: "Out of my/your/his mind" is an idiom. We already saw the explanation in the main book.

BY: A conversation can be an abstract path. "By the way" is a phrase. "The way" in this phrase means "now that you mention it, ...", but we can also use it with the meaning of "while we're talking, ..."

In the first case, we use the word "way" because you mention something which reminds me of some related detail or topic. That can take the conversation in a different direction (moving to a new and/or related topic). If a conversation can be an abstract path, then that path might split into different paths.

In the second case, we use the word "way" because you and I are having a conversation. While we're talking, (while we're on the path), I remember something or think of something that I want to mention. Here, "way" is just the conversation itself and not the topic because we're changing the topic completely. This is how the black cat uses the phrase "by the way". He's saying, "Because we're talking, I want to ask if you have any food because I'm hungry". The preposition "by" in both cases means "close to", but here it's very abstract.

WITH: If you have something while you're going somewhere, that thing is with you, so you and that thing are together.

ON: This is a strange case, but the preposition "on" also works in this sentence. Why? It's similar to the reason that we use the preposition "on" when we talk about wearing clothes. The clothes are on your body. If you're carrying an item with you (in your hand, in your pocket, etc…), then we can say that you have that item "on your person", which is an old phrase that we don't use much anymore. In fact, the biggest reasons why we don't use that phrase much is because we shorten it to "on you". Either way, think of it like a backpack. A backpack carries things and you put the backpack on your shoulders. We can easily say that the book that's in the backpack is "on" you because it's in the backpack. That's the basic idea. Having something "on you" is very loosely connected to the logic, or this might be a rare exception, but I think it still works.

"No, but I can give you some if you come **with** me **to** my house."
"You're going **to** take a talking cat home **with** you?"
"Sure. You can tell me **about** how you can talk **over** dinner. Anyway, I can't just leave you **out in** the cold."
"Yay! Let's go!"

WITH: Lena's going home. If the cat goes with her, they're together.

TO: "My house" is the destination.

TO: Ok, here we have the structure "going to do". We haven't talked about this one too much, but it's very logical. Why do we use the verb "to go" in the "-ing" form (in order) to express this meaning? Let's look at the pieces:

1) The basic meaning of the verb "to go" is "to move from one point to another point".

2) The continuous/progressive form ("-ing") describes a process.

3) So we have "the process of going", which is the process of moving from one point to another point.

4) If I say, "I'm going to the beach", this is the basic and normal use of the verb "to go" in the present continuous/progressive. I'm in the process of moving from where I was before/where I am now to the beach.

5) If I say, "I'm going to do it tomorrow", this is the use of "going" (in order) to talk about the future. Notice that because we're talking about a point in the future, we're not talking about a process anymore, at least not directly. Instead of pointing to a physical end point that I'm moving to (the beach), I'm talking about an action/verb. In English, when we use the preposition "to" (in order) to point to the second action/verb and connect it to "going", it creates the meaning of "future".

151

Think about it. If you're going to the beach, that's your destination. But if you're going to an action/verb, you can't physically go to it because it's not a location. However, it can be a point in time. And what period of time is after the present moment (now)? The future. **"_Going_ to do" is about _going_ forward in time** and doing the action at that time instead of now. So, I'm going to do it tomorrow means that the action will happen in the future, specifically "tomorrow".

I mentioned earlier that we're not directly talking about a process. We lose the feeling of a process, but it's still there in the background. There's a distance between the two points in time: the time I say the sentence (now) and when I do it in the future (tomorrow). Time is always moving forward, which means that as time passes, I'm moving forward with it. This means that I'm literally in the process of moving closer to the point in time when the I will do the action.

But there's one little detail here. The black cat asks, "You're going to take a talking cat home with you?" This doesn't seem like a point in the future. Another example: "Can you please take out the trash?" "Yeah, I'm going to do it right now". This example seems like we're talking about the present (right now). However, until the action actually starts, it's still in the future. "I'm going to do it right now" really means "I'm going to start doing it very very soon". So soon that it's almost in the present moment. This the same idea that's in the black cat's question. In the context of his question, we get an additional meaning: "Are you sure that you really want to do that?"

WITH: Lena and the cat will be going to her house together.

ABOUT: "To tell someone about something." We often use the preposition "about" with the verb "to talk" because whatever you're talking about is the scope/focus of your words. You can tell someone something, but that's different than telling someone about something. Sometimes these two are very close in real life and sometimes we can use them interchangeably. "Tell someone something" is a little more direct. "Tell me your

152

name." "Joshua." "Tell someone about something" puts a scope around "something": "Tell me about your name." "It originally comes from the Hebrew name "Yehoshua". The meaning is…"

When Lena says, "You can tell me about how you can talk", wants the cat to explain how it's possible that he can talk.

OVER: We saw the phrase "over dinner" in the main book.

OUT: This is short for "outside". "Out in the cold" simply means "without shelter", especially over night. It's a figure of speech (meaning that it's not literal), so you can use it even if it's not actually cold outside.

IN: "Out in the cold" is basically means "outside (of shelter) and inside the cold weather". That's the literal meaning, but remember that we don't have to use it literally. So, if you're "in the cold", "cold" or "cold weather" is the container, even if it's not actually cold. It's a container because instead of being inside shelter (like a house), you're in "nature", meaning whatever the natural environment outside is.

5) World War I

World War I (often abbreviated as WWI or WW1), also known as the First World War or the Great War, was a global war originating **in** Europe that lasted **from** 28 July 1914 **to** 11 November 1918.

IN: We know that the preposition "from" is an origin point, so why are we using the preposition "in" here? Because of the context. What this is saying is that the origin point was inside Europe. We're not talking about going from the origin point to some other point. Instead, we're talking about the location of the origin point, which in this sentence is inside Europe. "Europe" is a continent, which is bigger than a city or a country, so of course it's a container and we use the preposition "in".

FROM: Origin point in time.

TO: End point in time.

Described **at** the time as the "War **to** End All Wars", more than 70 million military personnel, including 60 million Europeans, were mobilized **in** one **of** the largest wars **in** history.

AT: During the time of the war, it was called "The War to End All Wars". So why do we use the preposition "at" instead of the preposition "in"? Again, it's the context. World War I is now history, and we can look at it as a point in time. It's not as specific as an hour ("at 9:00"), but we can look at a period of time as either a container or a point. Imagine a timeline that starts 2,000 years ago. Each event is a point on the timeline. A war is an event, so it's one point. However, that point can become a container if we go inside of it and look at the details. This is exactly the same as being at a store and going into it, except we're talking about time instead of space.

IMPORTANT AND INTERESTING NOTE: The timeline that we're talking about is a giant container of time (from 2,000 years ago to now). Inside that container, we put specific points on a line that goes through the whole period of the timeline. When we talk about a specific point, we're "at" that point. We can then go into that point. <u>So with our timeline, we have "in" → "on" → "at" → "in"</u>. But there's one more thing here. Notice that we say "a point **on** the timeline". When we're at a specific point (WWI), that point becomes a new container of time (28 July 1914 to 11 November 1918), which has it's own scale that goes through it that we can put specific points onto. More specifically, notice that when you zoom in or out between timelines, the scale changes. The first big timeline that started 2,000 years ago is one scale and now we're on a new scale. The specific point in time ("at") becomes a platform ("on"). So we have two possible paths, depending on how we want to talk about it and look at it: "at" → "in" and "at" → "on". The second "on" becomes the new scale and the second "in" becomes the new environment that we're talking about. So, in total we have 1) <u>"in" → "on" → "at" → "on"</u> or 2) <u>"in" → "on" → "at" → "in"</u>. If we combine these two (because the second "in" and the second "on" happen at the same time and it just depends on how we look at things), we have: **<u>"in" → "on" → "at" → "on" →</u>**

"in". Does that sound familiar? It's a perfect example of the Cone of Existence map in Appendix B of the main book.

TO: This is a great example of the logic of the preposition "to". WWI was such a big war that people thought it was impossible to have a larger war, or they thought that it was the biggest, most horrible war and that no other war would ever be bigger. "End All Wars" is the end point. "War" goes to that end point. "War" → "End All Wars", meaning that there will be no more wars after this one, at least not on such a large scale.

IN: Notice that the verb here is very important. The verb "to mobilize" means to organize and send soldiers to battle. So the soldiers are mobilized, but what are they mobilized in? Active groups.

OF: WWI is a part of the total number of large wars that have ever happened.

IN: History is a really big period (container) of time.

Over nine million combatants and seven million civilians died as a result **of** the war (including the victims **of** a number **of** genocides).

OVER: This means "more than".

OF: "Result" is part of the war. It's what happened by the end of the war and can include the effects afterward.

OF and OF: "A number" means "several or more". Let's make things easier. The word "victims" is connected to the word "genocides", but we have "a number" between these two. "Victims of genocide" is the idea here. The victims are part of the genocide. For example, we can also say, "The horrors of genocide", "the immorality of genocide", etc... In all of these cases, "genocide" is also the content, so it goes in both directions.

It was one **of** the deadliest conflicts **in** history and led **to** major political change, including the Revolutions **of** 1917–1923 **in** many **of** the nations involved.

OF: This is a part of the total number of deadliest conflicts.

155

IN: We saw this earlier.

TO: We saw this earlier. WWI led to major political change. In other words, major political change was the end point WWI (at least in this sentence).

OF: Many revolutions happened between the years 1917 and 1923.The revolutions were part of what happened in those years. This is the same as saying "the summer of 2009".

IN: This is "in nations". "Nation" is another word for country, and a country is so large that it's a container.

OF: This is "many of", which we've seen before.

Unresolved rivalries **at** the end **of** the conflict contributed **to** the start **of** the Second World War twenty-one years later.

AT: The end of WWI is a specific point in time. There were unresolved rivalries at that time.

OF: "The conflict" = WWI. A war has a beginning and an end, which are parts.

TO: We often use the preposition "to" with the verb "to contribute". This is because the action of contributing naturally points to the thing that you're contributing to. It's basically adding one thing to another thing, and the second thing is the end point.

OF: WWII (the Second World War) has a start and an end, which are parts.

The war drew **in** all the world's great economic powers, assembled **in** two opposing alliances: the Allies (based **on** the Triple Entente **of** the Russian Empire, the French Third Republic, and the United Kingdom) versus the Central Powers **of** Germany and Austria-Hungary. Although Italy was a member **of** the Triple Alliance alongside Germany and Austria-Hungary, it did not join the Central Powers.

IN: The verb "to draw" has a couple of different meanings. In this case, it's similar to the verb "to pull". There was a war and that war pulled all the great powers into itself. So the war is the container.

IN: "To assemble" means "to put together". In this case, we're putting together two alliances. An alliance is a kind of group, which is a container.

ON: Because the preposition "on" can be a surface or a platform, you can put things on top of that surface/platform abstractly. We talked earlier about how Newton built on Copernicus' work, which was the foundation for Newton's work. That's why we can say "based on". We're building on top of that surface/platform, which is usually a foundation of some kind. In this case, we're saying that the foundation/core of the group that was called "the Allies" was the Triple Entente.

OF: What's the content of the Triple Entente? In this case, what countries is the Triple Entente made of? Russia, France, and the UK.

OF: "A member of" = "a part of".

6) The Strange House

Two days ago, a friend and I were walking **at** night. We heard a strange sound coming **from** an old house. I've heard a lot **of** strange sounds **in** my life, but this was particularly strange. I can't describe it. My friend said that we shouldn't go **in**, but I wanted **to** because it seemed empty. I had **to** find **out** if something was inside or not.

AT: We saw earlier that the night is when most people sleep, so it seems like one big specific point that ends quickly.

FROM: The old house, most likely inside the house, is the origin point. The sound starts at that point and moves outward and away from it.

OF: "Strange sounds" is the content of "a lot".

IN: A lifetime is a container of time.

IN: This is short for "go inside (the house)" or "go into the house". A house is a building, which is a kind of container.

TO: This is the structure "want to do". Notice that we only have the words "want" and "to", which is all we need.

The action was just mentioned ("go inside"), so the preposition "to" points back to that action.

TO: This is the structure "have to do".

OUT: The phrasal verb "find out" is a little abstract. The meaning is "to discover" or "to learn", but in a particular way (for example, asking someone). First we have the verb "to find", so we're trying to find something. Then we have the preposition "out", which we know is 1) an outward direction or 2) the connection between "existence" and "non-existence", or the movement between two opposite containers. In this sentence, the person is saying that they want to discover if something is really inside the house. The truth of that is currently hidden. Once he finds the truth, it won't be hidden anymore and it will be "out", meaning "revealed" or "known". So we have the movement from the container "unknown" to the container "known".

We cautiously entered the house. The sound was louder inside. **For** some reason, it smelled like tea. Suddenly, we saw a blue light coming **from** a room **to/on** the right. My friend was nervous. He said we should leave, but I told him that there had **to** be a logical explanation and that we would be fine.

FOR: This is a basis, specifically a cause. "Some reason" means that the speaker doesn't know the reason. Specifically in this sentence, there's a reason (cause/basis) why the inside of the house smells like tea, but he doesn't know what that basis is. Is someone making tea? Does the house just naturally smell like tea? The most obvious answer is that someone is making tea, but the house seemed empty, so maybe there's another reason (cause/basis).

FROM: Inside the room is the origin point of the light. Usually, it comes from a light bulb specifically.

TO and ON: We talked about these two in the main book with the sentence, "The library is on the right (side)".

TO: This is the structure "have to do", but for probability instead of obligation.

158

To be honest, part **of** me wanted **to** leave. I wasn't sure if my friend was going **to** leave me there. I looked behind me and he was still there. Good. I slowly moved closer **to** the door. The sound stopped. I stopped. Even my heart seemed **to** stop. The door started **to** open. I couldn't move. I had **to** move! The door opened.

TO: We talked about "to be honest" in the book (preposition "to", group four).

OF: This is a part.

TO: This is the structure "want to do".

TO: This is the structure "going to do".

TO: "The door" is the end point and the person is moving closer to that end point.

TO: "Seem to do" works exactly the same way as "want to do", "have to do", etc...

TO: "Start to do" works exactly the same way as "want to do", "have to do", etc...

TO: This is the structure "have to do".

7) The Broken Heart

Today, Alex is reading **under/by** a tall, green tree. He's reading his favorite book, which has all **of** his favorite stories **in** it. The first story is **about** a man who has a horrible day. The second story is **about** a black cat. The third story is **about** a strange house.

UNDER: Alex isn't physically under the tree itself, meaning under the ground. If you sit under a tree, it means that the branches are over (above) you. Instead of saying "under the branches of a tree", we can simply say "under a tree" because it's obvious that's he's not under the ground.

BY: He can also be by the tree, which means near or possibly "next to" in this case.

OF: This is "all of", which we saw earlier.

IN: The stories are inside the book.

ABOUT X3: All three of these are talking about the topic/focus of the stories. You can also use the preposition "on", but the preposition "about" sounds a little better when we're talking about stories.

As Alex reads, something hits him **on/in** the head. He looks **down** and sees a small, white heart. It's broken. He picks it **up** and looks **around to** find whose heart it is. There's no one **around**. It's quiet. Alex goes home and brings the heart **with** him. That night, he fixes the heart.

ON and IN: We saw these in the main book. Your body is a surface and some other surface can hit it. When we're talking about bodies specifically, if the hit is soft, we use the preposition "on". If it's harder, we use the preposition "in" (in order) to show that there's more force.

DOWN: This is a downward direction.

UP: This meaning of "pick up" is literal. There's something on the ground, he grabs it, and lifts it up off of the ground. This is an upward direction.

AROUND: If you look around, you're vision moves in a circle or semi-circle as you look for something.

TO: This is "in order to". He's looking around so that he can find the owner.

AROUND: He's the central point. There's no one in the area where he is.

WITH: Alex and the heart are together as he goes home.

The next day, he comes back **to** the same place **with** the broken heart. Someone is **under/by/at** the tree. It's a mean, old man **with** a dog.

"Is this your heart?" Alex asks.

"No!" the old man says. "Go away!"

TO: "The same place" = the tree, which is the destination.

WITH: He has the broken heart with him, so they're together.

UNDER: This is the same as the previous "under".

160

BY: If we use the preposition "by", it can mean that the person is under the tree or just close to the tree. We know that most of the time when we're talking about specific locations, we can use the preposition "at" to talk about a very specific point and then the preposition "by" if we're talking about an area that's a little less specific, meaning that it's close to that specific point. When we do this, the preposition "at" is inside the area of the preposition "by". In this context, we're doing the same thing with the preposition "under" because that's still a specific point. We don't need the preposition "at" because the preposition "under" implies the preposition "at" in this context.

AT: The tree is a specific location.

WITH: The old man has the dog, so they're together.

So, Alex goes away and comes back later that day. A different person is **under/by/at** the tree. It's a young child.

"Is this your heart?" Alex asks.

"No." The child says.

Alex leaves again and comes back **in** the evening. He sees someone looking **around/under/by** the tree **for** something. It's a beautiful, young woman.

UNDER: Same as before.

BY: Same as before.

AT: Same as before.

IN: The evening is a large period of time during the day, so it's a container.

AROUND: We saw "looking around" earlier, but this is a little different. In the previous case, Alex was looking around ("look" + "around"). In this case, someone is looking for something ("look" + "for") and the place where they're looking is around the tree. The tree is the center point and there's an abstract circle around the tree that's a little larger than the area of the preposition "by".

UNDER: Again, this doesn't mean under the ground. The preposition "under" here is the same as the other ones,

161

except instead of sitting under the tree or being under the tree, someone is looking for something there.

BY: This is the same as the preposition "by" that we just saw, except now someone is looking for something and they're looking for it by the tree.

FOR: The person is trying to find something, so this is a purpose.

"Is this your heart?" Alex asks.

"My heart! You stole it!"

"No. It hit me yesterday when I was reading. I came back here **to** return it."

"Please give it **to** me."

Alex gives her the heart.

"Oh, I thought it was broken. Did you fix it?"

"Yes," Alex says.

The beautiful, young woman becomes very happy and falls **in** love **with** Alex.

TO: This is "in order to". Alex comes back (meaning "returned to the tree") so that he can return the heart to its owner.

TO: "Me" is the end point. In this case, the end point is a receiver.

IN: We talked about "in love" in the main book (group six). Remember that we naturally use the verb "to fall". This is because "love" is a container in this context. If it weren't a container, how could you fall into it?

WITH: We also talked about this in the main book. It's in the same explanation as the explanation for "in love".

8) <u>Language Learning</u>

Language learning is a big and complicated task **with** many different parts. A language isn't just one thing; it's a group **of** skills: speaking, listening, writing, and reading, as well as pronunciation. **Of** course, vocabulary and grammar are also big parts **of** learning a language. However, a grammar-based approach **to** language learning will usually fail. Grammar can be

162

useful, but trying **to** learn a language through grammar is like trying **to** learn how **to** ride a bike **by** reading a maintenance manual or studying physics. So where should you start?

WITH: Language learning is big and complicated and it <u>has</u> many different parts.

OF: There's more than one skill and they go into one big group. "Skills" is the content of "group".

OF: "Of course" is a very common expression that's actually short for "as a matter of course". The word "course" in this expression means "something that naturally happens or that is naturally/obviously true". The preposition "of" connects this idea to the information after the expression "of course". So this is a very strange case where the direction is broken, but the logic still works. Whatever information is after "of course" is the content of "course", or it can be a part of what happens or part of what is true.

OF: Vocabulary and grammar are parts.

TO: The verb "to approach" means "to move closer to something". In this sentence, we're using it abstractly and as a noun. We naturally use the preposition "to" because "language learning" is the end point. That's the task that you want to achieve and the approach itself describes how you're going to move forward so that you can achieve it.

TO: This is the structure "try to do".

TO: This is the structure "try to do".

TO: The structure "how to do" is very similar to "want to do", have to do", etc... We're using the word "how". As a question word, it means "in what way". When we use it in a statement (for example, "That's how you ride a bike"), it means "in that way". But there's something missing in this case. The structure isn't "how to do", it's "(action one) how to do". For example, "<u>Learn</u> how to ride" or "<u>Know</u> how to ride". Remember the special thing that we saw with the prepositions "about" and "to" (group three of the preposition "about")? This is similar, but instead of the preposition "about" between the verb "to be" and the preposition "to", we have the preposition "how" between the first action/verb and the preposition "to". So

163

this is like a combination between the "want to do" structure and the "to be about to do" structure, and it specifically focuses on the way that you do something. So, we have: "action/verb one" + "how" (way) + "to" + "second action/verb". Imagine there's a path or road. You want to know how to get to the next city. I point to that path. That path leads to the next city. Follow that path/go that direction (way) and you will reach the next city. "(verb) how to (verb)" works exactly the same. The word "to" connects the two verbs, and the word "how" shows the way (path) that they connect.

BY: "Reading a maintenance manual" and "studying physics" are the mediums through which you try to learn. They are the basis/source of your learning.

There are different opinions **on/about** this topic. **In** some people's opinion (**for** example, Steve Kaufmann (check **out** his YouTube channel)), you should start **by** focusing **on** listening and reading a lot. Other people, like Benny Lewis (also check **out** his YouTube channel), say the exact opposite: "Speak **from/on** day one!" Which one is better **for** learning a new language? It depends **on** you and how you prefer **to** learn.

ON: This is the topic that we're actively discussing, and the opinions go onto that topic as a platform.

ABOUT: This is another case where the prepositions "on" and "about" are interchangeable.

IN: When we say, "in my opinion", for example, I have my opinions about the world and specific things in the world, so whatever I think about something goes into the container called "opinions". Notice that we also have "in fact", which is used in a different way/context, but the logic is the same.

FOR: The information that's connected to the phrase "for example" is a basis and a purpose. It's a basis, because you're using that information as an example. It's a purpose, because you're giving that information for the purpose of explaining something.

OUT: We saw the phrasal verb "check out" earlier. "Check out his YouTube channel" means to explore his channel and see what's there.

BY: The structure "start by doing" means that there's a specific action that you should do (in order) to start. This is group two in the main book ("mode/method (more specific versions of "way"); a concrete (not abstract) medium"). It's similar to the sentence, "I learned how to sing by watching videos online."

ON: We've seen "focus on" many times. Remember that this is not a phrasal verb. The verb "to focus" usually uses the preposition "on" because it's simply logical most of the time. The thing that you focus on is like an abstract platform, but more importantly, it's the thing that is currently active in your mind. It's like you're shining the light of your conscious awareness onto that thing.

OUT: We already saw "check out".

FROM: Day one is the starting point in time. It means that on the first day that you start learning a language, you should start having conversations with people. "Speak from day one" is the Benny Lewis' catchphrase.

ON: "Speak on day one" is also possible, but 1) It's not Benny's catchphrase and 2) There's a slight difference in meaning. "On day one" just means that day. "From day one" means starting on that day and continuing to speak every day after that.

FOR: We're trying to find the method that is better if you want to learn a language. This can be a basis and a purpose. It's a basis because we're saying that if you want to learn a language (instead of how to program or swim, for example), then X is true. It's a purpose because we're trying to find which method is better so that we actually learn a language instead of wasting time.

ON: Remember that the verb "to depend" always or almost always uses the preposition "on". If something depends on you, then you're the surface/platform that we're putting the decision onto. For example, if you like the first method more

165

and it works better for you personally, then <u>based on</u> that, you should use the first method.

TO: "Prefer to do" works the same as "want to do", "have to do", etc... In this case, the meaning is close to "like to do". You have a preference and that preference points to the action of learning. "Prefer" + "to" + "learn".

It's true that we all learn a little differently. The traditional idea is that some people are "auditory" learners (listening-based), others are "visual" learners (sight-based), and others are "kinesthetic" learners (based **on** doing/physical use). These are partially true, but they don't matter because language learning is a group **of** four **to** five skills.

ON: "Based on" works because the thing that is the basis can be a platform/surface that we build on top of.

OF and TO: Notice that this is "of __ to __" instead of "from __ to __". Let's break this into smaller pieces. Language learning is a set of skills. How many? Four to five. We use the preposition "to" here because it depends on who you ask. Some people will say that the skills are speaking, reading, writing, and listening. However, other people (like me) say that there's one more skill: pronunciation. So we use the preposition "to" (in order) to show that there's a range of possible skills (4-5) instead of just one specific number of skills (4).

The preposition "of" works normally: "A group of four skills" ("four skills" is the content of "group"); "A group of five skills" ("five skills" is the content of "group"). We're simply combining these two into one sentence: "A group of four to five skills". "Four" is the starting point and "five" is the end point. The reason we use the preposition "of" instead of the preposition "from" is because the starting point is implied, but we need the preposition "of" (in order) to show that "four to five skills" is the content of "group". In other words, the exact content of "group" depends on who you ask.

For example, the skill **of** listening is, **of** course, listening-based. If you're a "visual learner", maybe you see the words **in** your head while you listen, and that's fine, but the point is that the only way **to** get really good **at** listening **to** a foreign language and understanding it is **to** listen a lot. **Of** course, knowing the language's pronunciation can help a lot, too, but even if you know all **of** the pronunciation rules, if you never actually listen **to** the language, you'll never be able **to** understand what you hear, especially when people speak quickly.

FOR: We've already seen "for example".

OF: We can say either "listening skills" or "the skill of listening" in this case. "Listening" is the content of "skill". What skill is it? Listening.

OF: We've already seen "of course".

IN: "In your head" means "in your mind". These two phrases are often interchangeable, but we're talking about the mind in this case. Your mind is the container in which you see the words.

TO: "The way to get" works similarly to "want to do", "have to do", etc... We're saying that there's a method that you can follow (in order) get (obtain) something. "Way" here is like an abstract path. If you follow that path, you will find what you want. In this case, you want to get something, meaning that you want an action. "Way" in this context is a path that leads to that action, and that action is the result because the action happens at the end of the path (the end point). Follow the path, get the result.

AT: This is the structure "good at", which we saw in the main book (group six). You want to improve your listening skills, which means that "listening skills" is the target. Check the main book for more details.

TO: We saw "listen to" earlier. Remember that "listen to" is more active and directed/focused while "hear" is more passive and unfocused.

TO: Idea 1: "the only way **to** get really good **at** listening **to** a foreign language and understanding it" = (is) idea 2: "listen a lot". We use the preposition "to" (in order) to point to the second idea, which is a verb. "X is" + "to" + "listen". We can

167

see that this is the same structure as "want to do", "have to do", etc… The only difference is that the verb "to be" isn't an action. The verb "to be" is basically just an equal sign (=), so we need something before it. Then we can use the preposition "to" if we want to point to an action as the second idea, which is what the first thing equals.

OF: We've already seen "of course".

OF: We've already seen "all of".

TO: This is "listen to".

TO: Notice that we can't you "can" in the future tense. Instead, we have to say, "will be able". When we use "can", we don't use the preposition "to" after it because "can" simply changes the mode of the verb, which like a special kind of conjugation. However, when we talk about being able to do something, we need the preposition "to". This is because "to be able" isn't a modal verb like "can". Because it's based on the verb "to be", we can conjugate it normally and use it in the present, past, and future tenses ("I am able to do", "I was able to do", "I will be able to do"."Can" and "to be able" have a very similar meaning, and many times, they're interchangeable, but in this case we have to use "to be able" because there is no form of "can" for the future tense. We use the preposition "to" because we're talking about an ability ("able") and that ability points to a particular action/verb.

Find All Possible Combinations

Instructions: Look at the list below. There's a list of all seventeen prepositions that we've been talking about. Your job is to choose all the prepositions that can work with each sentence below. There might be many possible answers. This exercise is similar to previous ones, but now we want to find all possible prepositions instead of choosing from a few. The purpose of this exercise is to think about all the possible contexts and meanings that a sentence can have depending on the preposition. If a preposition doesn't work, try to see if you can change the sentence a little to make it work. Write your answer. There are examples in the answers section. If you have any questions about your sentences, you can post them on italki or lang-8. Again, try to ignore answers that you think would be extremely uncommon. Note that for many of these sentences, there would be more answers if there were more information, especially after the last word in the sentence. We want to find the answers that work with the information that's there.

of, on, to, in, for, at, up, by, from, out, with, about, over, around, off, down, under

1) Put the book __ the desk.
2) Take the book __ the desk.
3) The food is __ me.
4) I want to get __.
5) She's walking __ the beach.
6) Throw it __.
7) Walk __ the store.
8) What is the book __?
9) Pull it __.
10) Move it __.

Answers and Explanations

1) Put the book __ the desk.

ON: A desk is a surface, so this means "on top of".

IN: A desk usually also has drawers, so you can put the book into one of them and we can simply say, "Put the book in(to) the desk".

BY: You can also put the book next to/close to the desk, so we can use the preposition "by". This usually means "on the floor next to the desk".

WITH: This one is possible, but it sounds like the context is that you're moving from one apartment to another apartment. The desk and the book are two of the items that you going to move, so you can put them together in the same place.

OVER: This means "above" and only works if you have a shelf or something else that is physically above the desk.

UNDER: Of course, you can also put the book in the space that's below the desk.

NOTE: In this context, "around" sounds a little weird unless you add some other words. For example, "Put the book somewhere around the desk". This is because the preposition "around" is a larger area than the preposition "by", so depending on the specific details of the context, we might need the word "somewhere", for example. We saw an example earlier: "Set all the books around the box", which means that you use the books to surround the box. In this case, however, we can't use that meaning because now we're only talking about one book.

2) Take the book __ the desk.

ON: This one doesn't work, but there's something important here. We often omit the word "that" between two clauses. For example, "I think that he's right". 99% of the time, we say, "I think he's right". This is also true with prepositions. You can't say, "Take the book on the desk". It doesn't make any sense. However, we can use "that is on" instead of just "on". For example, "Take the book (that is) on the desk". We almost never say "that is", but it's there in the background. This usually has

171

something else after it. For example, "Take the book (that is) on the desk and put it in the box".

TO: "The desk" is the destination.

BY: This one works, but if you use "(that is) by" and add something after "the desk", it can work.

FROM: This one works, but it will usually have something after "the desk". This is only because if I tell you to take the book from the desk, you're going to ask, "And do what with it?" If you use the preposition "from", it can have two meanings: "off of" and "out of". If the book is on the desk, you take it off (of) the desk. If the book is inside one of the drawers, you take it out of the desk. So in this case, the prepositions "from" and "off (of)" overlap and the prepositions "from" and "out of" overlap.

OUT OF: The preposition "out" by itself doesn't work, but if you add the preposition "of", it does. The reason for this is the same as in the previous examples where we saw "out of". Remember when Tom got out of the car? This is simply an outward direction from inside a container (the drawer of the desk). You can also apply the other part of the logic of the preposition "out", but it's not necessary here.

WITH: This one is uncommon, but it can work. This means that I'm giving you the desk and the book, so I want you to take both of them together.

OVER: "Take the book over the desk" doesn't make sense. If you mean "to the other side of the desk", then that's what we say: "Take the book to the other side of the desk". However, this is another example where you can use "(that is) over" and add something after "the desk".

AROUND: This is another way to say, "Take the book to the other side of the desk". The desk is the obstacle, like a fence.

OFF: Here, we don't need to use the preposition "of". It's optional and it's still there in the background. Of course, the logic here is that you're removing the book from a surface, which is the desk.

172

UNDER: Unlike the preposition "over", you can use the preposition "under" by itself. This is because you can physically take the book to the space that is below the desk (the floor) and then leave it there (it's more common to use the verb "to put", but "to take" can work here). However, "taking" the book to the space that's above the desk doesn't work. If you're putting the book on a shelf, then we say, "Put the book on the shelf (that's over the desk)" or "Put the book (on the shelf that's) over the desk". In other words, the verb "to take" combined with this context is why "over" doesn't work but "under" does work, and even then, as I said, "put under" works better than "take under" in this context. Of course, this can also mean "Take the book (that is) under the desk", which is usually followed by something else, like, "...and put it on the chair".

You can also use "(that is) under", meaning that the book is already under the table and you're going take it from there.

NOTE: The preposition "for" can work with the meaning of "exchanging one basis for another basis", but in this context, that seems extremely unlikely. Who would trade a book for a desk?

3) The food is ___ me.

ON: This has two meanings. The first meaning is simple: There's food and physically on me. Maybe someone threw food on me, for example. The second meaning is a little more complicated. If you say, "X is on me", it means that you're paying for it. Let's look at some examples.

You're at a restaurant with a friend and you're both eating lunch. When the waiter brings the check, your friend reaches for it, but you quickly grab it and say, "It's on me" or "The food's on me" or "The meal's on me". A similar example is when you're at a bar and the bartender gives you drink and says, "It's on the house!" "The house" means that the bar is "paying" for it. In other words, it's free. In both of these cases, we use the preposition "on" to show where the responsibility of payment is. That's like a weight that is put onto you.

FOR: If the food is for me, it means that the food was made for the purpose of me eating it. I'm the end point, but remember that a purpose is a special type of end point that we usually express with the preposition "for". For example, you go home and your brother sees that you bought a hamburger and fries. You also bought him a pair of shoes because he wanted a pair and you decided to get the food while you were out shopping. You're brother asks, "Can I have some?" You can say, "I bought you the shoes. The food is for me".

BY: This one isn't very common. Let's say that you cook food for your mother's birthday, but it's a surprise. You want it to taste good and look really nice, but you don't know how to make it look pretty. However, your brother knows how to put it on the plate and add some things that will make it look really professional and nice. When you surprise your mother, you might say, "The food is by me, the decoration is by Tom (your brother)". This is passive voice and you're the source of the food. This is part of group one in the main book.

FROM: You made or bought the food and sent it to someone or gave it to someone. You (or your money) is the origin point that the food came from.

WITH: You have the food with you and you're taking it somewhere (probably inside after you get out of the car). You and the food are together.

4) I want to get __.

ON: The most common situation where this works is when we're talking about amusement parks. "Get on" in that context means that you are boarding a ride. For example, a roller coaster.

IN: This is short for "inside" and it can be any container: a car, a big box, etc... The exact time that we would use this specific sentence depends on the context.

UP: Without any extra words (for example, "get up there"), this can mean that you're lying down or sitting down and something or someone is on top of you or holding you

174

down. "Up" in this case is simply an upward direction meaning that you want to stand.

BY: Someone is in the way and there's not a lot of room. For example, in a narrow hallway. This is similar to the sentence in group three in the main book: "He drove by us on his motorcycle".

OUT: You're inside something, like a car, and you want to exit. This is an outward direction.

OVER: Again, without extra information (for example, "over the bridge"), the meaning here is limited. The most likely use of this preposition in this sentence is when you're driving. If you're in one lane and you want to change lanes (move the car to the left or the right as you continue going forward), you have to move the car "over", meaning "to the side". Each lane is separated by a line or a series of broken lines. You're in one lane and you have to go over the line(s) if you want to change lanes. Notice that when we use this meaning of the preposition "over", we normally go from being <u>on</u> one side of something to being <u>on</u> the other side. In this case, we're going from being <u>in</u> one lane to being <u>in</u> another lane. That's one part of the meaning in this context. The other part is that "to the side" is like "to the east" and "to the west" when we're talking about a map/geography.

AROUND: This is like the preposition "by", and they're interchangeable in this kind of context (for example a narrow hallway where someone is in your way). We can use both because "by" means "past" and "around" means "moving forward and then to the side in a semi-circle (in order) to reach the other side of something".

OFF: You're on something (like a roller coaster) and you want to get off.

DOWN: This is not the opposite of "I want to get up". That would be "I want to sit (down)" or "I want to lie down". "I want to get down" means that you're up on top of something that's very high and you don't want to be up there. The context is very important. For example, if you're on a really big roller coaster and you want to get off, you might be bale to say "I want

175

to get down", but it's more about getting off of the ride completely. Instead, maybe you're on the roof of the house and then you realize that you're afraid of heights. "I want to get down" is probably most commonly used with and by small children. For example, the mother is carrying the child and the child says, "I want to get down", meaning that the child wants to walk instead of being carried.

5) She's walking __ the beach.

ON: The beach itself is the sand, which is a surface.

TO: The beach is her destination.

AT: Her location is the beach. This includes the area ("bubble") that we call "the beach", which is the water, the sand, the pier, and any places directly connected to it, like stores across the street.

UP and DOWN: A beach usually has a length that goes form one point to another point. If you walk along this point, you are going "up" and/or "down" the beach. The prepositions "up" and "down" depend on how you're thinking about it.

BY: She's close to the beach. This can have two meanings. 1) She's walking and the area that she's walking in is close to the beach, or 2) She's passing the beach, like the example in which the man passes by on a motorcycle.

FROM: The beach is the starting point and she's walking somewhere else.

AROUND: This can mean: 1) She's walking from one point to another point, but she's avoiding walking on the beach itself for some reason. She's trying to get to the other side. In this case, the beach is an obstacle. 2) She's on the beach or in the area that we call "the beach" and she's simply walking from place to place with no specific end point (destination) or no single end point (destination). This is like traveling around the world or the city. We're simply talking about the general area of something.

OFF: She's physically on top of the sand and now she's walking to a point that is off of the sand.

6) Throw it __.

ON: This can work in certain contexts. One context is clothing. You put clothes on your body. We can use the verb "throw" (in order) to show that you're in a hurry and/or that you don't care what you put on. Another context is with food. Let's say that you're making a really big salad or maybe a burger with lots of ingredients. "Throw it on" refers to the specific food that you're holding or talking about. The meaning is "to add", but when you add it, you throw it on top of what's already there. For example, "Throw some cheese on".

IN: Now we're talking about some kind of container. For example, you're going to sell somethings, and you're putting all of the things that you're selling into a big box. You have a shirt that you don't want, so you throw it in the box.

UP: This usually means an upward direction. Maybe you have a ball and you throw it straight up into the air, for example. It can also mean "to vomit", because "throw up" is the phrasal verb for that verb. Maybe you're sick so you don't want to eat anything because you're afraid that you'll throw it up.

OUT: "Throw out" is a phrasal verb that means "to throw away" (into the trash). There are a couple of other meanings, but that's the most basic and common.

OVER: You can throw something over a fence (from one side to the other). Or you can throw something on(to) someone so that it covers them. For example, you throw a blanket over your child. We don't literally "throw" the blanket, of course. Or you can throw your cup of coffee "all over" someone, which means you make the coffee fly out of the cup and onto them.

AROUND: This is very common with balls. If you're throwing a ball around, it just means "back and forth". There's no specific goal here. You're just throwing the ball (in order) to have fun.

OFF: This can be the opposite of "throw it on" when we're talking about clothing, or it can be the opposite of "throw it over" when talking about a blanket.

DOWN: This is a downward direction.

177

UNDER: This is simply throwing one thing so that it's now below something else. For example, you might throw a book under your desk. "Throw" isn't literal in this case. It gives us the idea of "quickly and without caring much". It's like saying, "Just put it under the desk".

7) Walk __ the store.
TO: The store is the destination.
IN: This can be short for both "walk into" and "walk inside".
BY: This means "close to" or "next to". The store is along the path that you're walking.
FROM: The store is the starting point.
OUT OF: You were inside the store and now you're outside of the store.
AROUND: This can mean 1) around the outside (circle); 2) around the outside, but stopping on the other side (front to back, side to side) (semi-circle); 3) You're inside the store and you're walking from point to point without a particular goal/target/end point. In other words, you're browsing, which means that you're simply looking to see what the store has and you might or might not buy something.

8) What is the book __?
ON: This can be the topic of the book (what the book is about), or it can mean that the book is physically on top of something. For example, a table.
IN: The book is inside a container, such as a box.
FOR: What's purpose of the book, or the purpose of having the book? Maybe it's for a specific class, or maybe you're friend gives it to you and want to know why he's giving it to you.
BY: This means that the book is next to/close to something.
ABOUT: This is the topic (scope) of the book.
UNDER: The book is physically under something else (maybe there's a box on top of it). Or if you're in a library, for

example, you're trying to find the book by category and you want to know what category the book is under. For example, "HISTORY".

NOTE: you might have chosen the prepositions "of" or "from", but these don't work here. They almost work, but we have to add a verb like "made": "What is the book made of?" and "What is the book made from?" This is mostly because we're asking "what" instead of "who" or "where", for example.

9) Pull it __.

ON: Without saying "onto something", the preposition "on" will most likely be used with clothes. If you put on clothes, usually a sweater/jacket or maybe a pair of pants, you can "pull it on", meaning you put it on(to) your body so that you're wearing it. It's more common to use the verb "to throw" in this context, but the verb "to pull" can work.

IN: You're inside something, like a room, and you're going to pull something into the room that's currently outside of the room. Note that in most cases you have to be inside the same space because we're using the verb "to pull", which means that you're moving it closer to you.

UP: This is pulling in an upward direction.

OUT: This is the opposite of "pull it in". You're outside of something and you're trying to pull something out that's inside something else. Note that we don't need the preposition "of" because we're not adding any other information. However, if you add the thing that it's inside, then we need the preposition "of": "Pull it out of the ground".

OVER: This can be many things. For example, when you go to bed, you pull a blanket over you. Or this can mean "to the side".

AROUND: This one is a little strange, but it works. A common context for this is when parking a car. For example, you want to park your car behind a building and you're currently in front of the building, so you pull (steer) the car around the building and park in the back.

179

OFF: Something is on top of something else and you're going to remove it. For example, you have a band aid on your hand because a cat scratched you and now you have to take the band aid off because your wound is healed. So you pull it off (of) your hand.

DOWN: This is pulling in a downward direction.

UNDER: Something is above something else and you want to pull it downward so that it's under that thing. This is commonly used when we're talking about water. For example, you're under the water and you want to see if you can pull a ball under the water with you and hold it there.

10) Move it __.

ON: The preposition "on" might work by itself in some cases, but usually you'll need to use "onto something". For example, "Move it onto the table". "Move it to (a place)" is also common, but again, we need some extra information, so it doesn't work here.

OFF: Again, this one probably isn't very common, but "off of something" works fine.

UP: This can be an upward direction, usually changing the position of something from a downward position to an upward position. It can also mean "forward" (in space) or "closer" (in space or time). For example, "I have to work on Monday, so I moved my doctor's appointment up (to today)".

AROUND: This just means to generally move something in a small area without any particular direction. For example, if you sit for too long, your leg might fall asleep (become numb). So you can get up and move it around (in order) to help the blood flow and regain the feeling in it.

ABOUT: This is the same as the preposition "around", but it's less common, at least in American English.

OVER: This means "to the side".

DOWN: This is a downward direction. Note that if we're talking about "away from" (in space or time), we use the preposition "back" here instead of the preposition "down".

180

Replace the Preposition

Instructions: Replace the underlined preposition in each sentence. Each preposition is correct, but you have to find another preposition that still works. However, <u>don't change the meaning</u>. In other words, you have to find a preposition that means the same thing in the context of the sentence. You might have to make a small change to the sentence, but avoid big changes.

1) "Do you travel a lot?" "Yeah, I travel all <u>around</u> the country."
2) His office is <u>up</u> this hall. It's the third door <u>to</u> the left.
3) Do you want to go <u>by</u> bus or <u>by</u> car?
4) It's stuck <u>in</u> the ground. I can't pull it <u>out</u>.
5) These days, you can access the internet <u>with</u> your phone.
6) Get <u>down from</u> that tree!
7) How can I do that <u>with</u> rules that are so strict?
8) Take it <u>out of</u> the box and put it on the table.
9) Children's toys these days are all made <u>of</u> plastic.
10) They covered themselves <u>in</u> mud (in order) to hide.

Answers and Explanations

1) "Do you travel a lot?" "Yeah, I travel all <u>around</u> the country."

AROUND → OVER: The preposition "around" in this context means "within the general area of specific point" (group three in the main book). This means that you don't have a specific end point (destination) or that you don't have a single end point (destination).

But we can also use the preposition "over" in this context. We know that the preposition "over" is about an arc-shape. We also know that we can use it with the meaning of the verb "to cover" (remember, "c" + "over"). This often happens when we also use the word "all": "all over". If you travel all over a country, it means that you've been to many places in that country, and those places are in different parts of the country. For example, in the US, maybe you've been to Los Angeles, New York City, Dallas (Texas), Miami, etc...

2) His office is <u>up</u> this hall. It's the third door <u>to</u> the left.

UP → DOWN: This is group five in the main book. It's that strange meaning that uses the idea of a "central platform" and basically means "away from" (down) or "closer to" (up). Remember that which preposition we use often depends on how we're thinking about it, but also where we are now in relation to our destination. In this case we have hall. Along the hall are the entrances to different room. If you say, "up this hall", then you're thinking about it from the perspective of the room ("office" in this case), which means that the person will walk closer to the room. If you say, "down this hall", then you're thinking about it from the perspective of your current location. The person who you're talking to is at the same location right now (let's say it's a desk in the front of the building). When the person walks closer to the room, they're walking away from the spot where you are, so we can use the preposition "down".

TO → ON: We've seen this many times before. Remember that when we have two sides, we can usually use either the preposition "on" or the preposition "to". For more information, see group one in the main book.

3) Do you want to go by bus or by car?

BY_1 → ON THE: Remember that we don't want to change the meaning here, otherwise there would be a lot of possible answers. When we use the preposition "by" in these cases, it's a little special. If we want to use another preposition, we need an extra word, often an article ("the"/"a"). The reason for this is because "by (transportation or communication)" doesn't use an article, but if we do use an article, the meaning changes. If I say "by the bus", it means "close to the bus", which is a different meaning of the preposition "by". We already know why we use the preposition "on": a bus is a large, special platform with the purpose of transporting many people.

BY_2 → IN THE: Of course, a car is a smaller, personal vehicle, so it's like a container. When we say, "I want to go in the car", it can mean 1) I want to enter the car (go inside), or 2) travel to the destination by car (driving).

4) It's stuck in the ground. I can't pull it out.

OUT → UP: If something is in the ground, then the ground is like a container instead of a surface. It's "holding"/"containing" that thing. Also if something is in the ground, then it's at a lower position than you. In other words, it's "down". When you pull it, you pull upward ("upward direction") so that it will come out of the ground.

IN → UNDER: The item doesn't have to be completely under the ground, but if you use the preposition "under", most of it or a lot of it is under the ground.

5) These days, you can access the internet with your phone.

WITH → ON: Of course, the preposition "with" here means "using". We saw the preposition "on" with things like computers, phones, and TVs in the main book (group four).

WITH → FROM: The device that you use (in order) to access the internet is an origin point/start point. If I access the internet from my computer, phone, tablet, etc…, then that's the origin point from which I load and view all the information that's online.

6) Get <u>down from</u> that tree!

DOWN FROM → OUT OF: In this sentence, we need both the prepositions "down" and "from". Also, if we use the preposition "out", this is another case where we also need the preposition "of". The reason that we need the preposition "from" and the reason that we can use the preposition "out" as an alternative is because we normally say that someone or something is <u>in</u> a tree. The area of the tree where all of the leaves and branches are is like a loose container.

DOWN FROM → OFF (OF): We can also use the preposition "off", but the meaning changes a little bit. It is possible to be on a tree, but now it sounds more like we're talking about the trunk of the tree. Ants and spiders, for example, can crawl on the tree. You might say the sentence, "Get off that tree!" if you're talking to a child who is try to climb it.

7) How can I do that <u>with</u> rules that are so strict?

WITH → UNDER: You want to or have to do something, but there are very strict rules that don't allow you to do certain things. This causes a problem. If we use the preposition "with", the thing you have to do and the rules are together, which makes the thing difficult to do. It's like someone is standing in your way and you don't know how to move forward.

If we use the preposition "under", the rules are pressing you down. This is kind of similar to the library example. Remember that the preposition "under" is a "downward force", which is often specifically the idea of "restricting". You can't do

185

certain things because of the rules, which means that rules restrict what you're allowed to do.

8) Take it <u>out of</u> the box and put it on the table.

OUT OF → FROM: If it's inside the box, of course the opposite in this case (and most cases) is "out of the box". But you can also use the preposition "from". It starts inside the box. You're going to take it from that point and put it on the table. Remember the tree from sentence six? The preposition "from" works the same way here.

9) Children's toys these days are all made <u>of</u> plastic.

OF → FROM: As we know, when we're talking about what something is made of, the prepositions "of" and "from" usually overlap and are interchangeable. The toy was originally just plastic and from that plastic, a toy was made.

OF → OUT OF: We can also sometimes often use "out of". This one is a little more abstract, but in this case, you take some plastic and "out of" that material a toy is the result. This is similar to taking something out of a box/from a box, but more abstract.

OF → WITH: The preposition "with" is also possible, but the meaning is a little bit different. "With plastic" can mean that the toy is made of plastic, but it might also mean that only some parts of the toy are made of plastic. It can also mean that the tools that were used (in order) to make the toys were made of plastic, but that's very unlikely in this case.

10) They covered themselves <u>in</u> mud (in order) to hide.

IN → WITH: The preposition "with" here means "using". "In mud" works because they're covering their bodies, but they not just putting in on their bodies. They're putting it all over their bodies. This makes the mud more like a container, kind of like how we can say that a man is "in a suit".

Notice that we can't use the preposition "over" here. This is partially because of the verb "to cover", but also because

186

that would mean that they use themselves to cover the mud, which is the opposite of what we mean in this sentence.

Prepositions in Real Contexts: Fix the Prepositions

Instructions: Earlier, you did the exercise that had stories or articles with blank spaces. This exercise is almost the same. Instead of blank spaces, some prepositions are correct and some are incorrect. You have to find the incorrect prepositions and replace them.

IMPORTANT NOTE: These are normal stories/articles, so there are other prepositions like "after", "through", "during", etc... Because we're only focusing on the logic of seventeen prepositions, the other prepositions are still in the text and you don't have to worry about them.

1) William Shakespeare

William Shakespeare was a British poet, playwright and actor. He is often called England's national poet, and the "Bard of Avon". His plays have been translated into every major living language, and are performed more often than those of any other playwright. Shakespeare was born and raised at Stratford-upon-Avon, Warwickshire. From the age of 18, he married Anne Hathaway, who he had three children with. Sometime between 1585 and 1592, he began a successful career over London as an actor, writer, and part-owner of a playing company called the Lord Chamberlain's Men, later known as the King's Men. Few records around Shakespeare's private life survive. (3)

2) The Weekend

A: What do you like to do in the weekends?
B: I usually stay in home and work on personal projects.
A: You mean like hobbies?
B: Yeah. I'm interested to many different things. Sometimes, I'll just work for hours and hours in one project, but other times, I jump around of one project to another.
A: Well, at least you stay busy.

B: What do you do at the weekends?
A: Me? I relax. Working hard in the entire week makes me really tired.
B: What do you do for relaxing?
A: It depends. Sometimes I go down to the beach, other times I stay to home and watch TV.

3) The Black Cat 2

Lena and the black cat continue talking.
"So, where do you live?" Lena asks.
"On the streets. I don't have a home."
"Strange. You're such a nice cat."
"Thanks. You're not bad of a human."
"So, where did you live before?"
"I used to live at a big, old, strange house with a strange human. He did a lot of strange things."
"Seems like the perfect place for a talking cat. Why did you leave?"
"I don't want to talk of it."
"Why? Was he mean?"
"Not exactly."
"Well, you can live with me if you want."
"Really? And you'll feed me everyday?"
"Yeah. I'll get some cat food and-"
"CAT FOOD?!"
"Yes, cat food. Or you can continue to live in the streets."
"But WHY?"
"Fine. I'll give you fish, but only once a week. Fish is expensive."
The black cat is sad. He looks at Lena with big eyes.
"Awww, so cute!" she says. "No."
"You're a bad human."
"And you're a bad cat."
"I like you," the black cat says. "The only thing that I ask is that you never get a white cat."
"Why? What's so bad from white cats?"

190

"If you have to ask, then I'm not going to tell you."
"Ok, I won't get a white cat. Happy?"
"Yes."

4) <u>News Report</u>

Over the news this week:

Millions of people are without power on the aftermath of the strongest earthquake from 100 years. Much of the city was damaged and the repairs are estimated for up $1,000,000.

The presidential election is coming over in a couple of months. The current president, who has been on office to four years, says that he won't run up reelection. He didn't say why, but many people think it's because in the battle over immigration reform, among other things. The country overwhelmingly opposed many of the president's policies, including everything of immigration to healthcare to economic policy.

A car crashed into the stage under a concert yesterday. Luckily, no one was killed, but about twenty people were injured, including one from the band members, who was thrown down the stage by the impact. The driver was driving under the influence and has been charged with drunk-driving.

5) <u>Vincent van Gogh</u>

Vincent van Gogh was a Dutch painter who is among the most famous and influential figures in the history in Western art. With just over a decade he created about 2,100 artworks, including around 860 oil paintings, most of them in the last two years in his life. They include landscapes, still lifes, portraits and self-portraits, and are characterized for bold colors and dramatic, impulsive and expressive brushwork that contributed over the foundations of modern art.

Born into an upper-middle-class family, Van Gogh drew as a child and was serious, quiet and thoughtful. As a young man he worked as an art dealer, often traveling, but became depressed after he was transferred to London. He turned under religion, and spent time as a Protestant missionary in southern Belgium. He drifted in ill health and solitude before taking out painting at 1881, having moved back home with his parents. His younger brother Theo supported him financially, and the two kept up a long correspondence to letter. His early works, mostly still lifes and depictions of peasant laborers, contain few signs of the vivid color that distinguished his later work. As his work developed he created a new approach to still lifes and local landscapes. His paintings grew brighter about color as he developed a style that became fully realized during his stay in Arles in the south of France at 1888. (4)

6) The Statue of Liberty

The Statue of Liberty is a giant sculpture in Liberty Island on New York Harbor at New York City, in the United States. The copper statue, a gift for the people of France to the people of the United States, was designed over French sculptor Frédéric Auguste Bartholdi and built by Gustave Eiffel. The statue was dedicated of October 28, 1886.
The Statue for Liberty is a figure of a robed woman representing Libertas, a Roman liberty goddess. She holds a torch above her head with her right hand, and in her left hand carries a *tabula ansata* inscribed in Roman numerals with "JULY IV MDCCLXXVI" (July 4, 1776), the date in the U.S. Declaration of Independence. A broken chain lies at her feet as she walks forward. The statue became an icon of freedom and of the United States, and was a welcoming sight to immigrants arriving by abroad. (5)

7) How Pronunciation Will Help You Learn English Better – Part 1

Having good pronunciation isn't just under your accent. In fact, pronunciation is probably the single most important thing that you can improve because it will help you improve almost all other areas in your English. That's why pronunciation is one of the core pillars of language learning. It's also why beginners should start training their pronunciation from day one and why a sound-first approach is so important. Let's take a closer look and learn more from how pronunciation will help you learn English (or any language) better.

Pronunciation actually has three parts. 1) Basic, individual sound units. For example, the "D" sound, the "R" sound, and the many different vowel sounds. This is what we usually think of when we hear the word "pronunciation". 2) Connections. This is about the flow between words (and sometimes inside words). For example, a common rule in English is what I call "nt + vowel". Look to this sentence: "I want it". We don't say "I" + "want" + "it". We say "I" + "wa" + "nit", or you can look at it like "I" + "wanit". Sometimes sounds are omitted between words and sometimes sounds change or combine between words. 3) Intonation.

8) How Pronunciation Will Help You Learn English Better – Part 2

English is a stress-timed language, which means that some syllables are reduced. Look at the sentence: "I want to go to the beach". The stressed words are "want", "go" and "beach" because these are the important content words. So the stress pattern on the sentence is "i WANT to GO to the BEACH." The other words are just grammar, so they are almost always reduced. The full pronunciation in the word "to", for example, is like the number "2". But normally, we don't say it that way. Instead, we reduce the vowel to a schwa and it sounds more like

193

"tuh".This is what a stress-timed language does, and it creates a very different rhythm and flow than a syllable-timed language.

All three of these (basic sounds, connections, intonation) are part of learning pronunciation and when I talk about pronunciation, I'm talking about all three of these things. That's why improving your pronunciation increases your listening ability, for example, because you're not just trying to hear basic sounds when someone is talking at you. You have to hear stress-patterns (intonation), which can change depending on the context (Is it a question? Are you implying how you feel about something? Etc...). You also have to be able to hear how sounds are connecting and/or changing between words. And you have to do all of this while listening for someone speak very quickly.

So, we can generally define pronunciation as being able to produce AND hear the exact sounds and rhythm of a particular language. Let's look more closely in listening specifically. This is probably the biggest benefit, especially around beginners and intermediate learners. Of course, you can just practice listening, learn more vocabulary and grammar, and other things. However, if you focus with improving your pronunciation first (or in the same time), your listening skills will improve a lot faster and more easily. But how and why does this work? (Continued in the next exercise...)

Answers and Explanations

NOTE: In order to save space in this book, I won't explain every preposition in this exercise. Instead, I only explain the ones that were incorrect. If you changed a preposition that was already correct, your answer might still be right. You can ask a friend or a teacher if those answers are correct or not.

1) William Shakespeare

William Shakespeare was a British poet, playwright and actor. He is often called England's national poet, and the "Bard of Avon". His plays have been translated into every major living language, and are performed more often than those of any other playwright. Shakespeare was born and raised ~~at~~ **in** Stratford-upon-Avon, Warwickshire. ~~From~~ **At** the age of 18, he married Anne Hathaway, who he had three children with. Sometime between 1585 and 1592, he began a successful career ~~over~~ **in** London as an actor, writer, and part-owner of a playing company called the Lord Chamberlain's Men, later known as the King's Men. Few records ~~around~~ **of** Shakespeare's private life survive.

    IN: Stratford-upon-Avon is a town in England.

    AT: We can use the preposition "from" with "the age of 18", but it's not right in this context. We're not talking about him starting something at the age of 18 and continuing to do it in the future (from that point and forward in time). We're talking about what he did at the age of 18 (get married).

    IN: London is a city.

    OF: "Shakespeare's private life" is the content of the records.

2) The Weekend

A: What do you like to do ~~in~~ **on** the weekends?
B: I usually stay ~~in~~ **(at)** home and work on personal projects.
A: You mean like hobbies?

B: Yeah. I'm interested ~~to~~ **in** many different things. Sometimes, I'll just work for hours and hours ~~in~~ **on** one project, but other times, I jump around ~~of~~ **from** one project to another.

ON: We know that we use the preposition "on" with days of the week. We don't usually use the preposition "on" with weeks. We usually just say "this week" or "next week", for example. However, when we talk about the weekend, we often do use the preposition "on". The weekend is two days, but notice that it the weekend, which is a singular word. This means that those two days are actually one big chunk of time between Monday and Friday. So, just like we can say "on Monday" or "on Saturday", we can also say "on the weekend". The weekend is active, just like a specific day like Monday or Saturday can be active. You can also look at it as a special abstract platform. But what about the week? We don't say "on the week". This is because the week is too long to be "on". Unfortunately, we don't say "in the week", either. We say "during the week". This is because we use the preposition "in" with the meaning "at the end of": "I'm flying to Japan in a week", for example.

Notice that in British English, they say "at the weekend". This is also perfectly logical, and it shows how different varieties of English have a little bit of a different "flavor". Imagine two people who are very similar. They're personalities are 97-99% the same, but there's that little difference. This also happens between dialects, but the preposition logic is mostly the same in all dialects. "At the weekend" works because it's the two days that are <u>at the end</u> of the week. Because the weekend is like one chunk of time, it's like one specific point in British English. But an American would never say that.

AT: Remember that when we talk about home, we usually talk about it as a location, so we use the preposition "at". It doesn't matter if you're inside or outside. If you have a specific reason to say if you're inside or outside, then the context is usually enough and we can simply say, "I'm inside",

196

for example. If you use the word "house", however, the preposition "in" and "at" both work and are equally common. It just depends on what you mean when you're talking to someone.

IN: We saw "to be interested in" in the main book (group five).

ON: We also saw "work on" in the main book (group three).

FROM: If you have many projects that you have to or like work on, then you can go from one project to another project. Let's say you work on your English for thirty minutes, then practice the guitar for an hour, then learn some Spanish for twenty minutes, then practice programming for a while, then do more English for twenty minutes, etc... The first project is the start point, the second project is the end point. When you go to the third project, the second project is the new start point and you go away from that to the new project, which is the new end point.

A: Well, at least you stay busy.
B: What do you do ~~at~~ **on** the weekends?
A: Me? I relax. Working hard ~~in~~ **for** the entire week makes me really tired.
B: What do you do ~~for relaxing~~ **to relax**?
A: It depends. Sometimes I go down to the beach, other times I stay ~~to~~ (**at**) home and watch TV.

ON: We saw this earlier.

FOR: This is a duration (length of time; group four in the main book).

TO relax: This is short for "in order to". The main reason that the preposition "to" works better here is that the preposition "for" sounds more like we're talking about a tool: "What's that for?" "It's for relaxing". Of course, in that case you can also say, "It's to help me relax".

AT: We saw this earlier.

197

3) The Black Cat 2

Lena and the black cat continue talking.

"So, where do you live?" Lena asks.

"On the streets. I don't have a home."

"Strange. You're such a nice cat."

"Thanks. You're not bad ~~of~~ **for** a human."

"So, where did you live before?"

"I used to live ~~at~~ **in** a big, old, strange house with a strange human. He did a lot of strange things."

"Seems like the perfect place for a talking cat. Why did you leave?"

"I don't want to talk ~~of~~ **about** it."

FOR: This one is a little tricky. It's possible to say, "You're not <u>that bad of</u> a human", but the meaning here is slightly different and we use it in a different context. Here, we use the preposition "for" because "human" is the basis (based on the fact that she's human and not a cat). The cat thinks that cats are better than humans, but the cat likes Lena. He's basically saying, "Well, you're a human, but despite that fact, I think you're ok".

IN: Notice that we're using the preposition "in" with the word "house". He lived in that house. When we use the word "home", a home is a location, even if it's not a building. For example, if you're from Mexico, you can say that Mexico is your home or that the city where you were born is your home. It's more about how you feel. However, a house is a building. Many times, a person's home is a house, but they're not the same thing.

ABOUT: We've seen "think about" many times. "Talk about" is very similar. Whatever you're talking about, that's the topic, which is the scope of your conversation. That scope can change over time as the conversation continues, but you can't talk about two things at the exact same time, at least not with the same person.

"Why? Was he mean?"

"Not exactly."

"Well, you can live with me if you want."

"Really? And you'll feed me everyday?"

"Yeah. I'll get some cat food and-"

"CAT FOOD?!"

"Yes, cat food. Or you can continue to live ~~in~~ **on** the streets."

"But WHY?"

"Fine. I'll give you fish, but only once a week. Fish is expensive."

The black cat is sad. He looks at Lena with big eyes.

"Awww, so cute!" she says. "No."

"You're a bad human."

"And you're a bad cat."

"I like you," the black cat says. "The only thing that I ask is that you never get a white cat."

"Why? What's so bad ~~from~~ **about** white cats?"

"If you have to ask, then I'm not going to tell you."

"Ok, I won't get a white cat. Happy?"

"Yes."

ON: 1) A car drives <u>on the street</u> because the wheels are supposed to touch the street (surface to surface). 2) A person walks <u>in the street</u> because they're supposed to walk on the sidewalk, which is usually raised compared to the street. This creates a small "valley" between the two sides of the street so the person walks in the street. 3) If you're homeless, you live on the street(s). This doesn't literally mean "on top of the street". It just means that the "street" is your only support. In other words, you don't have much, if anything at all. It's the only thing that you can metaphorically (not literally) stand on, meaning that the foundation of your life is very weak.

ABOUT: "White cats" is the scope and Lena wants to know what the bad thing is or what the bad things are inside that scope.

4) <u>News Report</u>

~~Over~~ **In** the news this week:

Millions of people are without power ~~on~~ **in** the aftermath of the strongest earthquake ~~from~~ **in** 100 years. Much of the city was damaged and the repairs are estimated ~~for~~ **at** ~~up~~ **over** $1,000,000.

     IN: It's possible to use the preposition "over", but it depends on the sentence. For example, "I heard it over the news". You can also use the preposition "on" in that case, but not the preposition "in". Why does it change like this? "On the news" means that it was the news that's on TV or on the radio. In other words, through communications systems (group four in the main book). "On the news" is just an extension of "on TV". "Over the news", like "on the news", is about the communications systems, so you can hear something over the news and it doesn't matter if you hear it through the TV, the radio, etc… However, we can also look at "the news" as a container that holds all the most recent information. Someone or something can be in the news, meaning that that person or thing is part of the news, just like if I have a pizza in a pizza box, each slice is a piece of the whole pizza, but they're all in one container (the pizza box).

     IN: "Aftermath" is usually the result of something really bad, like an earthquake. We say "in the aftermath" because that's the period of time after the event happens.

     IN: This is similar to what we've seen before with "in a minute", "in a couple of days", etc… We're talking about the result. Let's say there were 5 earthquakes in the last 100 years. Which one is the strongest? This one. The first one was about 100 years ago and was the strongest. It's not until 100 years later that a stronger earthquake happens.

     AT: "Estimated at" is a specific point of measurement.

     OVER: This means "more than".

The presidential election is coming ~~over~~ **up** in a couple of months. The current president, who has been ~~on~~ **in** office ~~to~~ **for** four years, says that he won't run ~~up~~ **for** reelection. He didn't say why, but many people think it's because ~~in~~ **of** the battle over immigration reform, among other things. The country overwhelmingly opposed many of the president's policies, including everything ~~of~~ **from** immigration to healthcare to economic policy.

UP: We saw an example like this in the main book ("up", phrasal verbs section)

IN: When someone is elected for a position a power (president, congress, etc...), we say that they are in office. "Office" here means their power and limitations, which is the container. For example, "the office of the president" doesn't mean an office room that the president uses. It's a slightly different meaning of the word. "In office" is basically the same as saying "in power", but only when elected. The power and limitations are the container because that container sets the boundaries of what they can and can't do from within that position of power.

FOR: This is a duration. He's been the president that long.

FOR: This is a purpose.

OF: When we say "because of", at least in this context, we're talking about "content" and not a "part". What's the content of "because"? In other words, what's (the content of) the reason?

FROM: We're saying that there are many policies that people oppose, which means that there's a wide range of policies that people oppose. We can start from one policy/issue, move to the next one, etc... When we say "from X to Y to Z", it just means that there are a lot of things involved and we're picking one random thing to start the list (in order) to show how wide the range is.

A car crashed into the stage ~~under~~ **at** a concert yesterday. Luckily, no one was killed, but about twenty people were injured, including one ~~from~~ **of** the band members, who was thrown ~~down~~ **off** the stage by the impact. The driver was driving under the influence and has been charged with drunk-driving.

AT: A concert is an event. We don't always use the preposition "at" when we're talking about events. For example, sometimes we use the preposition "in": "In the event that something bad happens, call me". That simply means "in case". However, when we use the preposition "at" with events, it's because we're talking about the location of the event. Where's the concert? Wherever it is, that's where the concert is located. The specific location in this sentence doesn't matter. We're simply talking about a car crashing into the stage. Where was the car and the stage when this happened? At the concert. We can also say that the car crashing into the stage is an event and we're talking about where that event happened. Both ways of looking at it work in this case.

OF: This is "one of", which we've seen many times already.

OFF: The meaning here is that the force of the impact that was caused by the car was so strong that the band member went from being on the stage to off of the stage. This is a surface and a platform, like we saw in the main book in the sentence, "He loves being on stage".

5) Vincent van Gogh

Vincent van Gogh was a Dutch painter who is among the most famous and influential figures in the history ~~in~~ **of** Western art. ~~With~~ **In** just over a decade he created about 2,100 artworks, including around 860 oil paintings, most of them in the last two years ~~in~~ **of** his life. They include landscapes, still lifes, portraits and self-portraits, and are characterized ~~for~~ **by** bold colors and dramatic, impulsive and expressive brushwork that contributed ~~over~~ **to** the foundations of modern art.

OF: This can be a part and content, but it's probably more content. The history of Western art is part of Western art,

202

but "Western art" is also the content. What history? Western art.

IN: This is exactly like "in a minute", "in a couple of days", etc… What was the result of the work that he did for over ten years? 2,100 artworks. Or we can say, how many works did he create by the end of that ten years? 2,100.

OF: This is also a common mistake that English learners make. The preposition "in" almost works, but it sounds a little weird in this sentence. One reason is because we already have the preposition "in": "most of them in the last two years". In this case, we want the preposition "of" because we're talking about when he created most of those artworks, which was during a period of two years, and those two years were part of his life.

BY: This is passive voice. The "bold colors and…" are what give the paintings their character.

TO: A contribution has an intended end point. What are you contributing to? Where is the contribution going? In this case, the end point is "the foundations of modern art", which means that his work helped create the basis of what we now call (the period of) modern art.

Born into an upper-middle-class family, Van Gogh drew as a child and was serious, quiet and thoughtful. As a young man he worked as an art dealer, often traveling, but became depressed after he was transferred to London. He turned ~~under~~ **to** religion, and spent time as a Protestant missionary in southern Belgium. He drifted in ill health and solitude before taking ~~out~~ **up** painting ~~at~~ **in** 1881, having moved back home with his parents. His younger brother Theo supported him financially, and the two kept up a long correspondence ~~to~~ **by** letter. His early works, mostly still lifes and depictions of peasant laborers, contain few signs of the vivid color that distinguished his later work. As his work developed he created a new approach to still lifes and local landscapes. His paintings grew brighter ~~about~~ **in** color as he developed a style that became fully realized during his stay in Arles in the south of France ~~at~~ **in** 1888.

TO: Because he was depressed, he was looking for answers. Where did you try to find them? In religion. He turned to religion because religion is the end point where he expected to find the answers. In other words, "religion" in this sentence is like an abstract destination. Note that this is a case where we can also use "look to" instead of "look at".

UP: The phrasal verb "take up" means "to start a new hobby". The preposition "up" in this case is about the idea of "creation", which also makes the hobby "active" (the connection to the preposition "on"). Why do we use the verb "to take"? Think of it like this: when you grab a pen, you're taking it, usually (in order) to use it. It's like the hobby is the pen.

IN: 1881 is the year in which he started painting.

BY: "By letter" is exactly the same as "by phone" and "by bus". Specifically, "by letter" means that they communicated through writing letters (not the alphabet; like e-mail, but on paper).

IN: Here we see the preposition "in" with "color". But this is a little different than the sentence, "Do you have this bike in green?" "Brighter in color" means that he started painting with ("using") brighter colors. We're using "color" as the container itself instead of the "color" being the color of the container (group three).

IN: The year 1888 is the container.

6) <u>The Statue of Liberty</u>

The Statue of Liberty is a giant sculpture ~~in~~ **on** Liberty Island ~~on~~ **in** New York Harbor ~~at~~ **in** New York City, in the United States. The copper statue, a gift ~~for~~ **from** the people of France to the people of the United States, was designed ~~over~~ **by** French sculptor Frédéric Auguste Bartholdi and built by Gustave Eiffel. The statue was dedicated ~~of~~ **on** October 28, 1886.

ON: We use the preposition "on" with islands because an island is a surface surrounded by water. This also makes it similar to a platform, but it's more a surface. Notice that when we talk about water vs land, we often say "in the water" and "on land". Of course, we can talk about a boat/ship being "in the water" (because part of it is inside the water) and "on the water" (because it floats on the surface of the water), but this is a special case.

IN: A harbor is basically a large body water where many ships leave and enter. But a harbor is more specifically an area made of water. Either way, you can see that we use the preposition "in" in this case.

IN: New York Harbor is part of the city, so we say that it's "in" in the city.

FROM: The gift wasn't for the people of France, it came from the people of France.

BY: "Was designed by" is passive voice. This is exactly like the sentence, "This book was written by my father" (group one), except instead of writing a book, we're talking about designing a statue.

ON: October 28th is the specific day. Remember that we use the preposition "on" with both days of the week (Monday, etc…) and days of the month (the 1st, the 5th, etc…). In this sentence, the focus is on the day that the dedication happened. The month and the year are important pieces of information, but we use the preposition "on" because that's the preposition that we use with days.

The Statue of Liberty is a figure of a robed woman representing Libertas, a Roman liberty goddess. She holds a torch above her head with her right hand, and in her left hand carries a *tabula ansata* inscribed in Roman numerals with "JULY IV MDCCLXXVI" (July 4, 1776), the date ~~in~~ **of** the U.S. Declaration of Independence. A broken chain lies at her feet as she walks forward. The statue became an icon of freedom and of the United States, and was a welcoming sight to immigrants arriving ~~by~~ **from** abroad.

OF: The Declaration of Independence has text, color, etc... "Date" is one part of it. When did it happen? That's part of the document.

FROM: The word "abroad" means "outside of a particular country". In this case, we're talking about the US, so "abroad" is every place that's outside of the US, specifically all other countries. Let's say that you're from China and you come to the US. You're coming to the US from abroad. China is the origin/start point that you leave from.

7) How Pronunciation Will Help You Learn English Better – Part 1

Having good pronunciation isn't just ~~under~~ **about** your accent. In fact, pronunciation is probably the single most important thing that you can improve because it will help you improve almost all other areas ~~in~~ **of** your English. That's why pronunciation is one of the core pillars of language learning. It's also why beginners should start training their pronunciation from day one and why a sound-first approach is so important. Let's take a closer look and learn more ~~from~~ **about** how pronunciation will help you learn English (or any language) better.

Pronunciation actually has three parts. 1) Basic, individual sound units. For example, the "D" sound, the "R" sound, and the many different vowel sounds. This is what we usually think of when we hear the word "pronunciation". 2) Connections. This is about the flow between words (and sometimes inside words). For example, a common rule in English is what I call "nt + vowel". Look ~~to~~ **at** this sentence: "I want it". We don't say "I" + "want" + "it". We say "I" + "wa" + "nit", or you can look at it like "I" + "wanit". Sometimes sounds are omitted between words and sometimes sounds change or combine between words. 3) Intonation.

ABOUT: If we say "about your accent", then "accent" is the scope. What this sentence means is that the scope isn't

206

limited to accent. There's more inside the scope. In other words, pronunciation is about more than just accent.

OF: As you know, we often use the preposition "in" with languages because they're containers. But containers have parts. In a language, there are the skills of speaking, reading, writing, listening, and pronunciation. Then we also have the areas of vocabulary and grammar. Those two aren't skills, so I just call them "areas". In this context, "skill" is a more specific word for "area". All of these skills/areas are part of the English language, so we can use the preposition "of".

ABOUT: Why do we say "learn about"? What you're learning is the focus, which can also be a scope. If you're learning about history, then you won't find much information about math because math is outside of that scope. In this sentence, we're going to focus the scope on "how pronunciation will help you learn English better".

AT: In this case, the sentence "I want it" is the target that I want you to "hit" with your vision.

8) How Pronunciation Will Help You Learn English Better – Part 2

English is a stress-timed language, which means that some syllables are reduced. Look at the sentence: "I want to go to the beach". The stressed words are "want", "go" and "beach" because these are the important content words. So the stress pattern ~~on~~ **of/in** the sentence is "i WANT to GO to the BEACH." The other words are just grammar, so they are almost always reduced. The full pronunciation ~~in~~ **of** the word "to", for example, is like the number "2". But normally, we don't say it that way. Instead, we reduce the vowel to a schwa and it sounds more like "tuh".This is what a stress-timed language does, and it creates a very different rhythm and flow than a syllable-timed language.

OF: Every sentence has different pieces: stress pattern (intonation), the pronunciation of individual sounds, and how those sounds connect, as well as other things, such as the letters (how the word is spelled), and even grammatical information, such as the subject, the verb, etc... So the stress pattern is one part of the sentence. Specifically, you can look at this as a characteristic of the sentence.

IN: The stress pattern is also in the sentence, so the sentence is a container that holds all of the information that we just saw.

OF: Every word also has different pieces. The pronunciation is one of them. Again, you can also say that this is specifically a characteristic of the word.

All three of these (basic sounds, connections, intonation) are part of learning pronunciation and when I talk about pronunciation, I'm talking about all three of these things. That's why improving your pronunciation increases your listening ability, for example, because you're not just trying to hear basic sounds when someone is talking ~~at~~ **to** you. You have to hear stress-patterns (intonation), which can change depending on the context (Is it a question? Are you implying how you feel about something? Etc...). You also have to be able to hear how sounds are connecting and/or changing between words. And you have to do all of this while listening ~~for~~ **to** someone speak very quickly.

TO: This is an interesting one. You might think that we should use the preposition "at" because the word "you" is the target. That's logical, but it's not quite how English looks at it. The person isn't trying to "hit" you and hurt you with their words. If they were, notice that we might something something like, "If someone throws insults at you, ignore them". When we say "talk to you", the person who's talking is communicating with you. You're the receiver of the message. In other words, you're the end point.

TO: We saw "listen to" earlier.

So, we can generally define pronunciation as being able to produce AND hear the exact sounds and rhythm of a particular language. Let's look more closely ~~in~~ **at** listening

208

specifically. This is probably the biggest benefit, especially ~~around~~ **for** beginners and intermediate learners. Of course, you can just practice listening, learn more vocabulary and grammar, and other things. However, if you focus ~~with~~ **on** improving your pronunciation first (or ~~in~~ **at** the same time), your listening skills will improve a lot faster and more easily. But how and why does this work? (Continued in the next exercise...)

AT: This is "look" + "at", but there are more words between them. It might seem strange to say "look at listening", but when we say "look at listening", it's implied that we're talking about the skill of listening and the details related to it.

FOR: This is a basis. It doesn't make much sense to think about this as a purpose, at least not directly. Based on the fact that someone is a beginner, or based on the fact that someone is an intermediate learner, that person will receive the most benefit.

ON: As you know, we almost always use the preposition "on" with the verb "to focus".

AT: Here's another example of the difference between the prepositions "in" and "at". In this case, we're not looking at "time" as a container. We're talking about doing two things at the same moment in time. It doesn't have to be literally at the same exact moment. In this case, it means that while you learn other things, you're also making sure that you improve your pronunciation. It's one activity among many, or it can be mixed with certain activities, like reading out loud instead of in your head.

Prepositions in Real Contexts: Add the Prepositions

Instructions: This is another exercise that uses stories/articles, but this time, all of the prepositions are missing. Add all of the prepositions that are needed.

This exercise is extremely difficult!
TIPS: Try to use the full context of the sentence and other sentences (in order) to find the answers. Some answers will be easy, some will be very difficult. Remember, sometimes there are two prepositions next to each other. Also remember that the verb is often important, even if it's not a phrasal verb. The first two articles are the hardest, so you can skip them and come back later if you want.

IMPORTANT NOTE: These are normal stories/articles, so there are other prepositions like "after", "through", "during", etc... Because we're only focusing on the logic of seventeen prepositions, the other prepositions are still in the text and you don't have to worry about them.

1) How Pronunciation Will Help You Learn English Better – Part 3

There are four basic skills language learning. Two them are producing the language (speaking and writing). This is called "output". The other two skills are understanding the language (listening and reading). This is called "input". There are many things that we can talk this topic, but that's not the focus here. There are also four other big areas language learning: pronunciation, vocabulary, grammar, and function.

We know that all these areas work together. Example, if you don't know any vocabulary, you can't understand anything that you hear. But pronunciation is special. When we think pronunciation, we think how you sound when you speak, which is output. However, there's a lot more it than just

211

sounding a certain way. Put it simply, **pronunciation is the bridge between input and output.**

When you were born, your brain could hear all the sounds that a human language can possibly have. Each language has its own set sounds, which might or might not overlap sounds another language, but your baby brain didn't care any the sounds that you didn't need your native language. So, as you started grow and your brain became familiar the sounds your native language, your brain focused learning how understand and produce the specific set sounds that your native language has. Sound – or more specifically, input – always comes first.

Now, I'm not saying that you have follow a strict listen-first, speak-later approach. As Polyglot Benny Lewis talks a lot, you can start speaking day one if you want, which has many benefits. What I am saying here is that pronunciation is much more important than most people think. It doesn't just help you speak more clearly and sound more natural, it also helps give your brain the tools it needs understand what it's listening. It's like food that you feed your brain so that it knows how use and understand the language. Other words, **pronunciation is both learning how say things AND learning how understand things**. Let's look some examples.

2) How Pronunciation Will Help You Learn English Better – Part 4

English, we have the letter "D", which is pronounced a certain way. Spanish, we also have the letter "D", which is pronounced a different way than the English "D". The English "D" is usually harder and stronger, where the Spanish "D" is softer and more like a mix between an English "D" and "TH". The exact placement the "D" sound both languages is also very different. So when a Spanish speaker looks the English word "do", they'll want pronounce it that soft Spanish "D". Likewise, when an English speaker sees the Spanish word "decir", they'll want pronounce it the harder English "D". Both cases, this creates an accent.

The problem is, both languages use the same letter ("D"), but the sound that that letter represents is different. So if your a native Spanish speaker, your brain is going try pronounce that sound when you're speaking English and hear that sound when you're listening English. Consonant sounds aren't usually a big problem, but vowel sounds are (a, e, i , o , u), especially when you're learning English.

Another example: look the image above. You can see the English letter "A" and the Japanese character " あ ". If we write Japanese words using English letters, this Japanese character (which is like a letter), is written "A". However, English, the letter "A" can represent several different sounds, but the Japanese " あ " only represents one specific sound. Addition, the "A" sound that Japanese speakers have is not a sound English. It's close the English sound that's words like "all" and "stop".

So when a Japanese speaker tries learn English or an English speaker tries learn Japanese, they both have learn how hear (and pronounce) a new sound that's slightly different than what they know their native languages. And they have do it the flow real speech. Remember that pronunciation isn't just creating the proper sounds, it's also being able hear the proper sounds. Your brain will try hear what it's used. So, part practicing pronunciation is getting your brain actually hear the new sounds without interference your native language. There are many things that can help you do this, including: minimal pair practice, shadowing, practicing front a mirror, and learning how feel what's happening inside your mouth.

Whatever you do, the point is that if you can't hear the sound, it's hard produce it. Likewise, if you can't produce the sound, it's hard hear it. When you train your brain hear new sounds, you might be able say those sounds more easily. It's a start because it helps be able hear the sounds first, but without active training, your pronunciation probably won't improve. However, the key is that **when you train your mouth produce new sounds, you'll be able hear them more easily, which improves your listening skill**. Reality, these two parts go together, but focusing more producing the sounds is a much quicker, easier, and more beneficial approach than focusing just hearing them. Remember: pronunciation is the bridge between input and output.

3) The Green Bike

Amy walks into a bike store. She's looking a new bike her son. She looks the store. There are many different bikes. Some are big, others are small; there are red ones, blue ones, white ones, and black ones. She doesn't know what get! Amy asks the store clerk what bike she should get her son.

"How old is he?" The store clerk asks.

"He's ten." Amy says.

"What color does he like?"

"He likes blue."

"Hmmmm… I don't know if we have any bikes blue. We're getting more bikes next week. You can come back then and see if we have any green ones."

"But there's a blue bike the window."

"Oh. That one's not sale. It's just display."

"I see. Well, why can't you put another bike the window?"

"I suppose I could, but I'd have ask my boss."

4) The English Language

English has developed the course more than 1,400 years. The earliest forms English, a set Anglo-Frisian dialects brought Great Britain Anglo-Saxon settlers the 5th century, are called Old English. Middle English began the late 11th century the Norman conquest England and was a period which the language was influenced French. Early Modern English began the late 15th century the introduction the printing press London, the printing the King James Bible and the start the Great Vowel Shift.

Through the worldwide influence the British Empire, Modern English spread the world the 17th mid-20th centuries. Through all types printed and electronic media, and furthered the emergence the United States as a global superpower, English has become the leading language international discourse and the *lingua franca* many regions and professional contexts such as science, navigation and law.

English is the third most spoken native language the world, after Standard Chinese and Spanish. It is the most widely learned second language and is either the official language or one the official languages almost 60 countries. There are more people who have learned it as a second language than there are native speakers. English is the most commonly spoken language the United Kingdom, the United States, Canada, Australia, Ireland and New Zealand, and it is widely spoken some areas the Caribbean, Africa and South Asia. (6)

5) Returning Home to New York

Steve is driving Adam's house. He's New York, but he just arrived California, which is the state that he currently lives. Steve calls Adam the phone as he gets closer the house.

Adam: Are you here yet?
Steve: Yeah, I'm driving your house right now.

Adam: Ok, I'll meet you front.

Steve: It looks like there's nowhere park.

Adam: Again? The neighbors usually invite people and they take all the parking spots.

Steve: It's ok, I'll find some place that's a little farther the street.

Steve drives a little while longer and parks the car an empty spot. He gets the car and walks back toward Adam's house.

Adam: Man, you had park all the way there? I'm sorry.

Steve: Don't worry it. How are you?

Adam: Good. It's good see you! So, how was the flight here?

Steve: Let's just say I'm glad be back the ground.

Adam: That bad, huh? Well, come and we'll have some coffee or something. So how's life California?

Steve: It's alright. Life there is pretty busy, though.

Adam: It's pretty busy here, too. This is New York!

Steve: Yeah, but it's a different kind busy, you know? Everyone is such a rush all the time. I'm thinking moving back here.

Adam: Really? Well, if you do, I have a friend who can get you an apartment cheap. It would be nice have you again.

6) Going to the Beach... or Not

Adam's walking the street Saturday afternoon. He lives Los Angeles, but he's visiting his friend Miami. His friend's busy, so he's going the beach himself, but he doesn't know how get there. As he walks, he sees someone. It's an old woman (who's) wearing a white hat. He asks her directions.

"Excuse me," Adam says.

"Yes?"

"Can you tell me how get the beach?"

"Yes. Just go this street until you see Main street and turn right."

"Thank you."
"You're welcome."

Adam goes the street until he sees Main street. He turns right, but he doesn't see the beach.
"Thief!" Someone says. Adam turns and sees the old woman. Suddenly, two police officers grab him.
"What are you doing?" Adam asks.
"You took that old woman's bag," one the police officers says.
"No I didn't! Do you see a bag?"
"I'm sure you have it somewhere."
"This is stupid!"
"You're coming us the (police) station."
Adam can't believe what's happening. He just wants go the beach and relax.

7) Creation of the United States

The history the United States began settlements Indigenous peoples before 15,000 BC. Numerous cultures formed. The arrival Christopher Columbus 1492 started the European colonization the Americas. Most colonies formed after 1600. the 1770s, thirteen British colonies contained 2.5 million people along the Atlantic coast east the Appalachian Mountains. After defeating France, the British government imposed a series new taxes after 1765, rejecting the colonists' argument that new taxes needed their approval. Tax resistance, especially the Boston Tea Party (1773), led punitive laws by Parliament designed end self-government Massachusetts.

Armed conflict began 1775. 1776, the Second Continental Congress declared the independence the colonies as the United States America. Led General George Washington, it won the Revolutionary War large support France. The peace treaty 1783 gave the new nation the land east the Mississippi River (except Canada and Florida). (7)

8) The Long Night

A: What are you doing?

B: I'm making coffee.

A: What are you making coffee? It's 11 night!

B: I have a lot work finish tomorrow.

A: If you stay all night, you won't get any sleep all. You should sleep least a few hours.

B: I will. I'll probably go bed 4.

A: Don't you have get 6?

B: Yeah. And then I have go the meeting present the project.

A: Don't you think you'll fall asleep the middle the presentation?

B: No. I'll be fine. But I'll probably pass when I get home.

Answers and Explanations

1) <u>How Pronunciation Will Help You Learn English Better –
Part 3</u>

There are four basic skills **in/of** language learning.
Two **of** them are **about** producing the language (speaking and
writing). This is called "output". The other two skills are **about**
understanding the language (listening and reading). This is
called "input". There are many things that we can talk **about**
on this topic, but that's not the focus here. There are also four
other big areas **of** language learning: pronunciation,
vocabulary, grammar, and function.

IN: The four basic skills are inside the concept/topic
called "language learning".

OF: Of course, each skill is one part of the concept and
process of "language learning".

OF: We've seen "one of them" many times. "Two of
them" works the same. There are four pieces (skills) in total
and we're talking about two of those pieces.

ABOUTX2: If you don't use the preposition "about"
in these two spots, it can work, but it sounds better with the
preposition "about". That's because we're talking about the
scope of the each skill. In this case, the scope of speaking and
writing is production and the scope of reading and listening is
understanding.

ABOUT: This is "talk about", so what comes after it is
the scope.

ON: Here's something interesting. We see the
prepositions "about" and "on" next to each other. This is why
it's very important to know what each preposition is connected
to in a sentence. The preposition "about" is connected to the
verb "talk": "talk about". The preposition "on" is connected to
the words "this topic": "on this topic". We already know how
the preposition "on" works when we're talking about a topic.
Just don't get confused here. The prepositions "about" and

"on" are clearly separate. They're simply next to each other in the sentence.

OF: Again, more parts. The four basic skills (areas/parts) are writing, reading, listening, and speaking. Then there are four other areas/parts: pronunciation, vocabulary, grammar, and function. So language learning is actually <u>made of</u> eight large parts.

We know that all **of** these areas work together. **For** example, if you don't know any vocabulary, you can't understand anything that you hear. But pronunciation is special. When we think **about** pronunciation, we think **about** how you sound when you speak, which is output. However, there's a lot more **to** it than just sounding a certain way. **To** put it simply, pronunciation is the bridge between input and output.

OF: This is "all of", which we've seen many times.

FOR: This is "for example", which we've seen many times.

ABOUT X2: These are "think about", which we've seen many times.

TO: We saw this structure before in the sentence, "There's <u>a lot to</u> learning a language <u>that</u> the average person <u>doesn't know</u>". In this case, however, we're saying that there's "a lot **more** to" something. In fact, in that example sentence, we can say, "There's a lot <u>more</u> to learning a language <u>than</u> the average person <u>knows</u>". These are two ways to say the same thing. In both cases, we're using the "a lot to something" structure. The sentence "There's a lot more **to** it than just sounding a certain way" works the same.

TO: This is actually short for "in order to", but it works a little differently. This is part of group four in the main book. It works exactly like the phrase, "To be honest, ..." We're using the preposition "to" (in order) to point to the action. That's all we need. I'm pointing to the action "put", which is connected to "it simply". Together, we get "put it simply". So I'm pointing to the phrase "put it simply" because I want to tell you that what comes after this phrase is the general idea of what I'm saying. I can't just say, "Put it simply", because that's a command. So the preposition "to" let's you know that I'm pointing to "put it simply". In other words, I'm directing your attention to the main/general idea.

When you were born, your brain could hear all **of** the sounds that a human language can possibly have. Each language has its own set **of** sounds, which might or might not overlap **with** sounds **in/of** another language, but your baby brain didn't care **about** any **of** the sounds that you didn't need **in/for** your native language.

OF: This is "all of", which we've seen many times.

OF: "Sounds" is the content of "set", which is a more specific word for "group".

WITH: "Overlap" means that two things share the same area. Part of each is in the same area, but the rest of each is outside of that area. For example, Russian and Spanish have the same "A" sound, so that sound overlaps in these two languages. But there are sounds in Russian that don't exist in Spanish, so those sounds don't overlap because they're different, so they're outside of that shared area. The preposition that we usually use with the verb "to overlap" is the preposition "with". This is because of the shared area. Certain sounds are together when we compare the two languages, but other sounds are separate because those sounds only exist in one of those languages.

IN and OF: Again, a language is often a container. The sounds of a language are part of it, but they're also inside it.

ABOUT: We've seen "think about", "talk about", etc... Here we have "care about", which works the same way. If you care about something, it's important to you. That thing is the scope/focus of what's important.

OF: This is "any of", which works the same as "all of". The difference is that "all" means "every" (100%) and "any" means "an unspecific one".

IN: "Native language" is the container.

FOR: We can also use the preposition "for" here. This is "for the <u>purpose</u> of speaking and understanding your native language".

So, as you started **to** grow and your brain became familiar **with** the sounds **of** your native language, your brain focused **on** learning how **to** understand and produce the specific set **of** sounds that your native language has. Sound – or more specifically, input – always comes first.

TO: This is "start to do".

WITH: We often use the preposition "with" with the word "familiar". You have a familiarity and that familiarity is connected to something. The familiarity and the thing go together.

OF: Sound is one part of a language.

ON: Here we have "focus on" again.

TO: This is the structure "how to do".

OF: Again, the sounds are the content of "set".

Now, I'm not saying that you have **to** follow a strict listen-first, speak-later approach. As Polyglot Benny Lewis talks **about** a lot, you can start speaking **from** day one if you want, which has many benefits. What I am saying here is that pronunciation is much more important than most people think. It doesn't just help you speak more clearly and sound more natural, it also helps give your brain the tools it needs **to** understand what it's listening **to**. It's like food that you feed your brain so that it knows how **to** use and understand the language.

TO: This is the structure "have to do".

ABOUT: This is "talk about".

FROM: "Day one" is the starting point. Of course, as we saw before, we can also use the preposition "on", but Benny Lewis' phrase is "Speak from day one".

TO: Ok. Here we have "need" and the preposition "to", but this is not "need to". Remember, we need to know what words the preposition is connected to when trying to find the logic. This is actually "in order to". "The tools that it needs" for what? Why does it need those tools? In order to understand.

TO: In this case, we can either say "listening to" or "hearing". The two verbs overlap in this context because we're talking about the brain. Can we simply say, "...to understand what it's listening"? No. In this case, the preposition "to" is necessary, even though we're not saying something after, like "listening to <u>music</u>". But why? It's possible to say, "...to understand what it's hearing". Now we're using the more "passive" verb "to hear", so we don't need the preposition "to". But if we use the verb "to listen" in this case, we need the preposition "to" so that we can point back to the word "what". Remember words like "what" and "that" are placeholders that refer to pieces of information. "<u>What</u> are you listening <u>to</u>?" "I'm listening <u>to</u> <u>music</u>."

TO: This is the structure "how to do".

In other words, pronunciation is **about** both learning how **to** say things AND learning how **to** understand things. Let's look **at** some examples.

IN: We know that we often use the preposition "in" with languages, and that includes words. This is because languages are mostly made of words. The words are the container that we put our thoughts into so that we can communicate those thoughts with someone. We naturally use the preposition "in" in the phrase "in other words" because that phrase means that I'm going to repeat what I just said, but in a different way. I'm changing the container (the words) so that I can explain more clearly and/or simply.

ABOUT: What is the scope of "pronunciation"? What's its focus? "Learning how to say things and learning how to understand things". The scope isn't only centered on learning how to say things. The scope is learning how to say things AND understand them.

TO: This is the structure "how to do".
TO: This is the structure "how to do".

223

AT: As we know, the verb "to look" usually uses the preposition "at" because the thing that you're looking at is the target of your vision (or the target of your conscious attention). In this case, the examples are the target.

2) How Pronunciation Will Help You Learn English Better – Part 4

In English, we have the letter "D", which is pronounced **in** a certain way. **In** Spanish, we also have the letter "D", which is pronounced **in** a different way than the English "D". The English "D" is usually harder and stronger, where the Spanish "D" is softer and more like a mix between an English "D" and "TH". The exact placement **of** the "D" sound **in** both languages is also very different.

IN: English is a language, which is a container.

IN: We use the preposition "in" with the phrase "in a certain way", because "way", closely related to the idea of "direction", can be a container. This might seem strange, but remember that the context is very important.

IN: Spanish is a language, which is a container.

IN: Same as before.

OF: Here we're talking about where you put your tongue inside your mouth so that the "D" sound is created. A sound can have a strength (hard or soft), a volume (loud or quiet), etc... "Placement" is one part of the sound. More specifically, it's part of how we create the sound.

IN: "Both languages" means English and Spanish, which are containers.

So when a Spanish speaker looks **at** the English word "do", they'll want **to** pronounce it **with** that soft Spanish "D". Likewise, when an English speaker sees the Spanish word "decir", they'll want **to** pronounce it **with** the harder English "D". **In** both cases, this creates an accent.

AT: This is "look at".

TO: This is the structure "want to do".

WITH: When a Spanish speaker pronounces the "D" sound, they use a soft "D".

TO: Same as the previous "to".

WITH: Same as the previous "with".

IN: A "case", meaning a "situation" or a "circumstance", is a container that holds the events, results, or other information about something.

The problem is, both languages use the same letter ("D"), but the sound that that letter represents is different. So if you're a native Spanish speaker, your brain is going **to** try **to** pronounce that sound when you're speaking English and hear that sound when you're listening **to** English. Consonant sounds aren't usually a big problem, but vowel sounds are (a, e, i , o , u), especially when you're learning English.

TO: This is the structure "going to do".

TO: This is the structure "try to do".

TO: This is "listen to". Remember that we use the preposition "to" because you're actively directing your hearing to something, and that thing is the end point.

Another example: look **at** the image above. You can see the English letter "A" and the Japanese character " あ ". If we write Japanese words using English letters, this Japanese character (which is like a letter), is written "A". However, **in** English, the letter "A" can represent several different sounds, but the Japanese " あ " only represents one specific sound. **In** addition, the "A" sound that Japanese speakers have is not a sound **in** English. It's close **to** the English sound that's **in** words like "all" and "stop".

AT: This is "look at".

IN: Language is a container.

IN: When you add things, you're adding things into an equation. For example, $2 + 2 = 4$. We start with one "2", then we add another "2" into the equation. If you add another "2" into the equation, the answer is six. When we're talking about information instead of math, we have the phrase "in addition".

What we're doing is we're adding more information into the information that we already have. So the total amount of information is the container, which means that this is a special case, but the logic still works.

IN: Language is a container.

TO: If you're "close to" something, it means that you're location/position is a short distance from the location/position of some end point.

IN: Words, which are part of language, are containers.

So when a Japanese speaker tries **to** learn English or an English speaker tries **to** learn Japanese, they both have **to** learn how **to** hear (and pronounce) a new sound that's slightly different than what they know **from/in** their native languages. And they have **to** do it **in** the flow **of** real speech.

TO: This is the structure "try to do".

TO: This is the structure "try to do".

TO: This is the structure "have to do".

TO: This is the structure "how to do".

FROM: The native language is the starting point/origin point of their knowledge. Based on that knowledge, they have to learn something that's similar but a little different.

IN: Because languages are usually containers, their knowledge can also be in that language, just like the words. In this context, this can also be short for the idea of knowing about something that is part of their native language.

TO: This is the structure "have to do".

IN: A "flow" is something that you can be inside. Think of a river, for example. You're in the water, but that water is also flowing ("moving") in a certain direction. So you're also inside that flow. When people speak, there's a certain rhythm and speed. This is what we call the "flow of speech". Different languages use different rhythms and speeds depending on the context and other things, so this also connects to the larger idea of being "in a language".

OF: "Flow" is part of "real speech".

226

Remember that pronunciation isn't just **about** creating the proper sounds, it's also **about** being able **to** hear the proper sounds. Your brain will try **to** hear what it's used **to**.

ABOUT: The scope of pronunciation isn't only creating sounds.

ABOUT: The scope of pronunciation is also hearing sounds.

TO: This is the structure "able to do". Instead of using the modal verb "can", we usually have to use "be able to" after a preposition. This is because we have to use the "-ing" form of a verb if the verb is after a preposition, but modal verbs like "can" don't have an "-ing" form.

TO: This is the structure "try to do".

TO: Here we see the preposition "to" at the end of the sentence and attached to the structure "be used to doing". Remember that this is not past tense. This structure means that you are accustomed to something. In other words, it's something that's normal for you. In this case, there are certain sounds that are normal for your brain to hear and understand. These are the sounds of your native language. Until your brain adjusts to the new sounds of the language that you're learning, it will try to hear and understand only the sounds that it knows based on your native language.

So, part **of** practicing pronunciation is getting your brain **to** actually hear the new sounds without interference **from** your native language. There are many things that can help you do this, including: minimal pair practice, shadowing, practicing **in** front **of** a mirror, and learning how **to** feel what's happening inside your mouth.

OF: This is "part of".

TO: This is a nice and useful structure: "to get someone/something to do something". The verb "to get" in this structure means "to force" or "to achieve". For example, if you're playing soccer ("football"), you try to get the ball into the goal. When we say "getting your brain to actually hear the new sounds without interference", it means that you're trying to force your brain to hear the actual sounds, or you're just trying to achieve that goal.

We use the preposition "to" in this structure because we're saying "force" ("get) + someone/something + "to" + "do". In this case, the word "to" connects the action of forcing and the second action. It points to that second action successfully happening through force.

FROM: Where does the interference come from? What's the origin/source of the interference? Your native language.

IN and OF: This is "in front of", which is a chunk. Remember that the opposite is usually "behind", but "in (the) back of" exists and we use it in certain contexts. Why do we use the preposition "in"? There's the <u>front part of</u> something and the <u>back part of</u> something. If you're "in front of" something, it means that the space that you're body occupies right now is the space that's related to the front part. Obviously you're not inside the front part of that thing. For example, if you're in front of a mirror, it doesn't mean that you're inside the mirror's front. It means that you're inside the space that is located directly in front of the mirror. The context makes this clear. If you're in front of a store, it's the same: you're in the space that's outside of the store and related to the front part. If you want to say that you're <u>inside</u> the store related to the front part, you have to use the word "the": "I'm <u>in the front of</u> the store".

TO: This is the structure "how to do".

Whatever you do, the point is that if you can't hear the sound, it's hard **to** produce it. Likewise, if you can't produce the sound, it's hard **to** hear it. When you train your brain **to** hear new sounds, you might be able **to** say those sounds more easily. It's a start because it helps **to** be able **to** hear the sounds first, but without active training, your pronunciation probably won't improve. However, the key is that when you train your mouth **to** produce new sounds, you'll be able **to** hear them more easily, which improves your listening skill.

TO: We've seen structures like "want to do", "have to do", and "how to do". Here we have the structure "to be hard to do". It works exactly the same. We're saying that something is difficult, and the difficulty points to the action/verb.

TO: Same as the previous one.

TO: This is "train to do". The verb "to train" means that you force someone or something (including yourself) to reinforce/practice an action. We simply use the word "to" (in order) to connect the verb "to train" and the action that you're reinforcing/practicing.

TO: This is "able to do".

TO: This is "helps to do".

TO: This is "able to do".

TO: This is "train to do".

TO: This is "able to do".

In reality, these two parts go together, but focusing more **on** producing the sounds is a much quicker, easier, and more beneficial approach than focusing **on** just hearing them. Remember: pronunciation is the bridge between input and output.

IN: "Reality" is a container. This is closely related to the logic of the preposition "out" when we talk about the containers of "existence" and "non-existence".

ON: This is "focus on". Remember, when you focus on something, that thing is active in your awareness. In this context, it's also closely related to "work on" because you're practicing producing the sounds, which is a form of work.

ON: Same as the previous one.

3) The Green Bike

Amy walks into a bike store. She's looking **for** a new bike **for** her son. She looks **around** the store. There are many different bikes. Some are big, others are small; there are red ones, blue ones, white ones, and black ones. She doesn't know what **to**

229

get! Amy asks the store clerk what bike she should get **for** her son.

FOR: This is "looking for", which means "searching for". In both cases, the logic can be a purpose and a basis. It can be a purpose because there's a reason that she's trying to find something. It can be a basis because she's trying to find something based on certain information. In this case, that information is that her son wants a bike, so that's the basis of her search. This sentence is more about a basis than a purpose, but both work.

FOR: The purpose of buying the bike is to give it to her son.

AROUND: This is part of group three in the main book, which is "within the general area of a specific point".

TO: Earlier, we saw "(action one) how to do". This is almost the same, but now we're using the word "what" instead of the word "how". This means that we're not talking about the way to do something, we're talking about what to do. In other words, what is the second action or what should you do with the second action? In this case,"What bike should I get?"

FOR: This one is the same as the previous "for".

"How old is he?" The store clerk asks.
"He's ten." Amy says.
"What color does he like?"
"He likes blue."
"Hmmmm… I don't know if we have any bikes **in** blue. We're getting more bikes next week. You can come back then and see if we have any green ones."
"But there's a blue bike **in** the window."
"Oh. That one's not **for** sale. It's just **for/on** display."
"I see. Well, why can't you put another bike **in** the window?"
"I suppose I could, but I'd have **to** ask my boss."

IN: This is just like the sentence, "Do you have this bike in green?" (Group three) It's important to note that there are times when we can use the preposition "of" with colors. Obviously we can say something like, "The color of this wall

230

is ugly", but what I'm talking about is "clouds of white". For example, there's a famous song by Louis Armstrong called, "What a Wonderful World". In that song, he says, "I see trees of green" and later in the song he says, "I see skies of blue and clouds of white". We would never say "trees in green", "skies in blue", or "clouds in white", so the "in" version doesn't work at all because we simply don't talk about it that way, but the "of" version works because it sounds very poetic. It's not how people normally talk.

IN: We saw "in the window" in the main book (group two). In this case, there's a bike which is probably on a special little platform so that people can easily see it through the window.

FOR: If something is "for sale", then the purpose of that thing is to sell it to someone.

FOR: If something is "for display", then the purpose of that thing is just to show it to people.

ON: We also saw "on display" in the explanation of the sentence, "There's a sign (that's hanging) in the window" (group two in the main book).

IN: This is the same as the first "in".

TO: This is the structure "have to do".

4) <u>The English Language</u>

English has developed **over** the course **of** more than 1,400 years. The earliest forms **of** English, a set **of** Anglo-Frisian dialects brought **to** Great Britain **by** Anglo-Saxon settlers **in** the 5th century, are called Old English. Middle English began **in** the late 11th century **with** the Norman conquest **of** England and was a period **in** which the language was influenced **by** French. Early Modern English began **in** the late 15th century **with** the introduction **of** the printing press **to** London, the printing **of** the King James Bible and the start **of** the Great Vowel Shift.

OVER: Remember, when we're talking about a period of time, we can often use the preposition "over", especially if

231

it's a really long period of time. This is like "over the winter", which we saw in the main book (group six).

OF: "Over the course of (X amount of time)" is a chunk. The amount of time can be a day, a week, a month, a year, etc… "The course" just means "throughout". In other words, we're talking about the entire period of time. In this case, it's a length of 1,400+ years. "Course" is part of the amount of time, but we can also say that the amount of time is the content of the course. Is it a day, a week, a year?

OF: There have been many different forms of English. The oldest is Old English, then Middle English, and now we have Modern English. These are the large labels. There are also many smaller details, but that doesn't matter here. All these forms have been part of the English language over time, and "English" is the content of "forms". Notice that because "forms" is plural, the content actually changes (Old English, etc…)

OF: This is "set of". "Anglo-Frisian dialects" is the content of "set".

TO: We have the verb "to bring" (past tense: brought), which is a verb of motion. The earliest forms of English weren't spoken in Great Britain (the UK). When the people who spoke those dialects moved to Great Britain, they brought the language with them. "Great Britain" is the destination (end point).

BY: There are a lot of words here. The simple version is "brought by Anglo-Saxon settlers". This is passive voice. The Anglo-Saxons were the medium through which Old English entered the area that we now call (Great) Britain/England.

IN (X2): A century is a container of time because it's so big. Remember, "at 9:00", "on Monday", "in May", "in 1999", "in the 90's", "in the 20th century".

WITH: The Norman conquest of England was the event that started the change from Old English to Middle English. This is because the Normans were French, and this is the period where French had a huge influence on the English language. We can use the preposition "with" in this case because the two events are together. More specifically, the Norman conquest indirectly "brought" the change with it.

OF: We can definitely say that the conquest is part of England's history, but it might be strange to say that it's part of England itself. However, we can see that "England" is the content of "conquest". When one group conquers another group, the conquered group is the content of the conquest. For example, "conquest of England", "conquest of the Americas", "conquest of India".

IN: This is "in which". More specifically in this sentence, "a period in which". The word "which" is a reference for the word "period" (of time), which is a container. Note that we don't always need the preposition "in". It depends on what you're saying. For example, "The 17th century, a period which is one of my favorites, was very interesting." Notice when I say "a period which", I'm not talking about something happened in that period, I'm just talking about the period itself. However, when we're talking about England in the example sentence, we're talking about French influencing English during that period, so we need to use the preposition "in" with the word "which".

BY: "Was influenced by" is passive voice. French is the language through which the influence/changes happened. If it were Japanese, for example, then that influence/change would have happened through Japanese.

IN: A century is a container of time because it's so big.

WITH: The printing press, the King James Bible, and the Great Vowel Shift were things that happened at the same time as the creation of Middle English, so they all go together.

OF: An introduction (similar to a "beginning") is part of something. The printing press was still new and it was just being introduced to England.

TO: Where was the printing press introduced? What was the end point? London. You might think that we should use the preposition "in" here. That can work, but the preposition "to" works much better, at least in this sentence.

"The introduction of (thing) to (place)" is a standard structure. The reason that the preposition "to" works better here is because the thing was outside of that place but now it's brought into that place. Notice if I say, "I'd like to <u>introduce</u> you <u>to</u> my friend, Tom", w use the preposition "to". Who or where is the introduction directed to?

OF: "The King James Bible" is the content of what was printed, but you can also say that the printing was part of the book. A book has a cover, a font, a number of pages, etc… If it's printed, then that printing is part of the book.

OF: This is "start of", which is a part of something.

Through the worldwide influence **of** the British Empire, Modern English spread **around** the world **from** the 17th **to** mid-20th centuries. Through all types **of** printed and electronic media, and furthered **by** the emergence **of** the United States as a global superpower, English has become the leading language **of** international discourse and the *lingua franca* **in** many regions and professional contexts such as science, navigation and law.

OF: "Influence" is part of "the British Empire". Note that we can also say "the British Empire's influence".

AROUND: This can be "in a circle", but it's more about "something that's within the general area of a specific point" (group three). More specifically, we're talking about "from place to place with no specific destination".

FROM: This process started in the 17th century.

TO: This process ended in the mid-20th century.

OF: "Type of" works the same as "kind of". Notice that we're also saying "all", so this is "all of" + "type/kind of".

BY: What helped to spread English even farther? What helped make English such a popular and influential language? The power and influence of the United States. This use of the preposition "by" is group one ("an abstract medium that's a cause/source") because the additional <u>source</u> ("furthered by") of English's influence is the US.

OF: There's the US and then there's the US as a global superpower. This is one chunk. The US already existed before it was a global superpower, so it had already "emerged" (started). Later, the US became a global super power. That status has a beginning, which is what "emergence" means in this context. You can think of it as "the start of the US's global power". So, "emergence" is part of "the US as a global superpower".

OF: "Leading language" is part of "international discourse". The language in which people interact is only one part. The things that people talk about is another part, for example.

IN: "Regions" are large areas, and an area is usually a container. A context is also a container that holds all the details of what's happening, even if it's not directly said. Details include location, body language, formality levels, etc...

English is the third most spoken native language **in** the world, after Standard Chinese and Spanish. It is the most widely learned second language and is either the official language or one **of** the official languages **in/of** almost 60 countries. There are more people who have learned it as a second language than there are native speakers. English is the most commonly spoken language **in** the United Kingdom, the United States, Canada, Australia, Ireland and New Zealand, and it is widely spoken **in** some areas **of** the Caribbean, Africa and South Asia.

IN: This is "in the world", which we saw earlier.

OF: This is "one of", which we've seen many times.

IN: A country is a very large area, so it's a container.

OF: Every country has at least one official language. "Official language" is part of a country. What language(s) do they speak there?

IN: These are all countries, which are containers.

IN: In this case, we're not talking about countries, we're talking about "some areas". An area is a container.

OF: Which areas? What are the areas part of? The Caribbean, Africa and South Asia. We're not saying that English is spoken everywhere in the Caribbean, Africa and South Asia (all areas/parts). We're saying that it's spoken in some areas. An area is usually a container, but a container can also be a part of some larger thing. In this case "The Caribbean, Africa and South Asia" are large areas and we're breaking those large areas into smaller areas, which are parts of the larger areas.

5) Returning Home to New York

Steve is driving **to** Adam's house. He's **from** New York, but he just arrived **from** California, which is the state that he currently lives **in**. Steve calls Adam **on** the phone as he gets closer **to** the house.

TO: The house is the destination (end point).

FROM: Steve was born in New York, so that's where he's from. That's his origin point.

FROM: He lives in California, not New York. So he's originally from New York, but now we're saying that he just arrived from California to New York. California is the origin/starting point of his trip and New York is the destination/end point.

IN: He lives in California. A state is such a large space that it's a container.

ON: This is "on the phone". Remember that phones are part of the communications system, which is a platform for communicating.

TO: This is the structure "closer to". In this case, we're simply talking about getting closer to his destination, which is Adam's house, so the preposition "to" points to that end point.

Adam: Are you here yet?
Steve: Yeah, I'm driving **up to** your house right now.
Adam: Ok, I'll meet you **out** front.
Steve: It looks like there's nowhere **to** park.

Adam: Again? The neighbors usually invite people **over** and they take **up** all the parking spots.

Steve: It's ok, I'll find some place that's a little farther **up** the street.

UP: This can mean an "upward direction", but that doesn't matter. Remember that the preposition "up" can mean "moving closer to" something. That's what it means in this case. More specifically, notice that it's not just "up to your house", it's also "right now". This is because we usually use this when we're very close the destination.

TO: The house is the end point.

OUT: The phrase "out front" is another way to say "in front of". "I'll meet you in front of the house". "I'll meet you out front". We don't say, "out front of the house", because (in order) to use this phrase, the thing that you're in front of (the house in this case) is implied. But why out? We know that the preposition "in" works because you're in the space/area that is located directly in front of the house. The preposition "out" also works in this context because you're meeting someone outside of the house, but you're also in front of the house. We combine these two ideas and simply say "out front".

TO: Steve wants to park his car. He needs a place/spot to park it, so he's looking for somewhere to park. He doesn't see any near Adam's house, so there's nowhere to park that's close to the house. The preposition "to" points to the action/verb "park", but it's also pointing to a possible parking spot, which is the end point that he's trying to find.

OVER: This is the same as "go over to someone's house" or "come over (to my house)". The only difference here is that we're using the verb "to invite": "invite (someone) over".

UP: The phrasal verb "take up" has a few meanings, but in this case it means that all the parking spots are gone because there are cars in all of the spots. The cars are <u>taking</u> the spots. The preposition "up" emphasizes the idea of "completion". The preposition "up" is optional in this case and you can simply say, "They take all the parking spots."

237

UP: Here you can use the preposition "up" or the preposition "down". The preposition "down" obviously works because you're moving farther away from the house. However, the preposition "up" also works here because you can think about it as getting closer to the empty sparking spot that you're driving to.

Steve drives **for** a little while longer and parks the car **in** an empty spot. He gets **out of** the car and walks back toward Adam's house.

FOR: This is duration (length of time), which is the third part of the logic.

IN: The words "spot" and "space" are very similar, but it depends on the context. In this context, they're interchangeable. So, just like you can be inside of an area or a space, you can also be inside of a spot. More specifically, a parking spot.

OUT OF: He was inside the car, which is a container, and now he's outside of the car.

Adam: Man, you had **to** park all the way **down** there? I'm sorry.
Steve: Don't worry **about** it. How are you?
Adam: Good. It's good **to** see you! So, how was the flight **out** here?
Steve: Let's just say I'm glad **to** be back **on** the ground.

TO: This is the structure "have to do".

DOWN: Notice the meaning of "away from". This is emphasized with the phrase "all the way". What Adam is saying is that the closest parking spot that Steve could find is far away from the house (maybe 2-3 blocks).

ABOUT: As you know, we use the preposition "about" with the verb "to worry" or "to be worried" because your worry has a specific scope.

TO: "To be good to do something" is another structure in which the word "to" connects two actions/verbs. In this case, we have "to be good". "To be" isn't a dynamic verb (action),

238

it's a stative verb (state of being). However, we can still use the word "to" if we want to connect "to be" and another action/verb. What's good? A specific action/verb. Which action/verb? "See". "It is good" + "to" + "see you".

OUT: The preposition "out" is optional in this sentence. We can add it to emphasize the distance between where Steve was and where he is now. In this case, that means the distance between California and New York. From California, you have to travel a long distance away. This is the same as "out in the country".

TO: Again, we see "to be" used with the word "to", but now we're saying "to be glad" + "to" "be back".

ON: He flew from California, but he didn't like the flight, so now he's glad to be back on top of a solid surface that's not in the air, which is the ground.

Adam: That bad, huh? Well, come **in** and we'll have some coffee or something. So how's life **in** California?
Steve: It's alright. Life **out** there is pretty busy, though.
Adam: It's pretty busy here, too. This is New York!
Steve: Yeah, but it's a different kind **of** busy, you know? Everyone is **in** such a rush all the time. I'm thinking **about** moving back here.
Adam: Really? Well, if you do, I have a friend who can get you **in** an apartment for cheap. It would be nice **to** have you **around** again.

IN: This is short for "into (the house) or "inside". Both of these can work here, but "into" is the main idea.

IN: California is a state, which is a container.

OUT: Again, we can use the preposition "out" because California is very far away from New York. Adam could have asked "How's life out in California". Notice that we still need the preposition "in", but we can also add the preposition "out" (in order) to emphasize the distance.

OF: This is "kind of", which is about content.

IN: The phrase "to be in a rush" or "to be in a hurry" means someone is trying to go somewhere or finish something really quickly. "Rush" is a very abstract container and this phrase is very idiomatic, so it might seem really strange. This could be a rare exception to the logic.

ABOUT: This is "think about".

IN: This is short for "into'. "To get someone in(to) an apartment" means to help that person find an apartment and be accepted into the apartment by the managers/owners. Adam is saying that his friend can help Steve with that or that his friend knows someone who can help Steve with that.

TO: Again, we find "to be" with the word "to". "It would be nice" + "to" + "have you around".

AROUND: The phrase "to have someone around" means that the person lives in the area, which means that you can visit them, hang out with them, do things with them, etc… The preposition "around" simply means "in the area". In other words, the two people live in the same area, usually the same city, even if it's a big city.

6) Going to the Beach… or Not

Adam's walking **down/up** the street **on** Saturday afternoon. He lives **in** Los Angeles, but he's visiting his friend **in** Miami. His friend's busy, so he's going **to** the beach **by** himself, but he doesn't know how **to** get there. As he walks, he sees someone. It's an old woman (who's) wearing a white hat. He asks her **for** directions.

UP/DOWN: We've seen this many times. All of the details are in group five of the preposition "down" in the main book.

ON: Notice that we say "in the afternoon", but "on Saturday afternoon". This is actually short for "on Saturday in the afternoon", but what we're talking about is very clear, so we can omit the words "in" and "the". Saturday is the active day, and it can also be an abstract platform.

IN X 2: Los Angeles and Miami are cities, which are containers.

TO: "The beach" is the destination.

240

BY: As we saw in the main book: "If you do something 'by yourself', you do it alone. We use the reflexive pronouns (yourself, myself, etc..), and that's the key here. Whatever action it is, it happens <u>through</u> your own efforts without the help of someone else. In other words, you are the path through which the action happens. We can easily see how you are also the cause/source of that action." This is the same as the sentence, "She's old enough to walk home by herself" (group one in the main book).

TO: This is the structure "how to do".

FOR: This is a purpose because his question has a purpose: to get directions to the beach.

"Excuse me," Adam says.

"Yes?"

"Can you tell me how **to** get **to** the beach?"

"Yes. Just go **up/down** this street until you see Main street and turn right."

"Thank you."

"You're welcome."

TO: This is "how to do". The verb "to get" in this context means "arrive at/reach".

TO: "The beach" is the destination.

UP/DOWN: This is the same as the previous UP/DOWN explanation.

Adam goes **up/down** the street until he sees Main street. He turns right, but he doesn't see the beach.

"Thief!" Someone says. Adam turns **around** and sees the old woman. Suddenly, two police officers grab him.

"What are you doing?" Adam asks.

"You took that old woman's bag," one **of** the police officers says.

"No I didn't! Do you see a bag?"

"I'm sure you have it somewhere."

"This is stupid!"

"You're coming **with** us **to** the (police) station."

241

Adam can't believe what's happening. He just wants **to** go **to** the beach and relax.

UP/DOWN: This is the same as the previous UP/DOWN explanation.

AROUND: Adam is facing one direction. He turns 180 degrees and is now facing the opposite direction. This is a semi-circle.

OF: This is a part (two total, one is speaking).

WITH: Adam and the police officers are going to the police station together.

TO: "The police station" is the destination.

TO: This is the structure "want to do".

TO: "The beach" is the destination.

7) Creation of the United States

The history **of** the United States began **with** settlements **by** Indigenous peoples before 15,000 B.C.E. Numerous cultures formed. The arrival **of** Christopher Columbus **in** 1492 started the European colonization **of** the Americas. Most colonies formed after 1600.

OF: "History" is a part of the United States. The US has a population, a size/area, laws, religions, geography, history, etc...

WITH: What was the first event that started the history of the US? Settlements by indigenous peoples. The start and the event go together.

BY: Who started the settlements? Indigenous peoples. Through their act of settling, the history of the US began. Of course, it's actually just part of the history of North America, but we're going as far back in time as possible to when people first started living in what we now call the United States.

OF: This is an example of when we can use the preposition "of" or the apostrophe "s" ('s): "The arrival of Christopher Columbus" or "Christopher Columbus' arrival" (of course, in this case, we just use the apostrophe because the name ends with the letter "s"). So this is an example where the preposition "of" contains the idea of "possession", but remember, that's not the key idea of this preposition.

But how does the preposition "of" work here? Christopher Columbus arrived. The noun form of the verb "to arrive" is "arrival". His arrival. The arrival isn't part of him, but it is part of what he did (go to the Americas). It's like "his car". The car isn't part of him, it's part of what he owns.

IN: A year is a container.

OF: You can look at this as a part (specifically part of the history of the Americas), but this is more about content. "The Americas" is the content of "colonization". If a group colonizes an area, then that area is the "content" that is colonized. This works the same as "the Norman conquest of England".

By the 1770s, thirteen British colonies contained 2.5 million people along the Atlantic coast east **of** the Appalachian Mountains. After defeating France, the British government imposed a series **of** new taxes after 1765, rejecting the colonists' argument that new taxes needed their approval. Tax resistance, especially the Boston Tea Party (1773), led **to** punitive laws **by** Parliament designed **to** end self-government **in** Massachusetts.

BY: This means "not later than".

OF: This is a "part" because if we start at/from the Appalachian Mountains, there are areas to the east, to the west, to the north, and to the south. We're talking about the coastal area that is to the east. That area is "part" of all the areas (to the east, west, north, south) around the Appalachian Mountains.

OF: "A series of" is similar to "a number of", but in a particular order.

TO: This is "led to".

BY: Parliament created the laws. They are the abstract source that the laws came from (group one in the main book).

TO: This is short for "in order to". The purpose of the laws was to remove the ability of the people to govern

243

themselves. In other words, the laws were designed for that purpose.

IN: Massachusetts is a state in the US. In 1773, it wasn't a state yet. It was a colony, but a colony is a container, even if it's not very big. This is because "colony" is like a special version of the word "group".

Armed conflict began **in** 1775. **In** 1776, the Second Continental Congress declared the independence **of** the colonies as the United States **of** America. Led **by** General George Washington, it won the Revolutionary War **with** large support **from** France. The peace treaty **of** 1783 gave the new nation the land east **of** the Mississippi River (except Canada and Florida).

IN X 2: These are the years, which are containers.

OF: This is a part. The colonies had money, populations, land, resources, sizes, etc…

OF: This one might seem weird, but "America" is the content of "United States". Let's look at another example: Many people don't know this, but Mexico is officially called "The United States of Mexico" because Mexico is actually a group of multiple areas that are called "states", just like the US. Notice that we normally just say "Mexico", and this is also true when we're talking about the US: we either say "the US" or "America".

Of course, you can also look at this as a "part". There are many states, which in this context is like many parts that the country is made of. So the country is "America", but it has many states (parts) which are united into one country. Now we can see that this is like a pizza: one whole pizza, many pieces/slices (parts).

BY: We've seen "led to", but what about "led by"? The preposition "to" is the most common and basic preposition that the verb "to lead" uses, but we can also use the preposition "by". Who led the military forces during the Revolutionary War? George Washington. The sentence is actually passive voice, but with the structure of the rest of the sentence, we

244

can't say the first part as "The military forces were led by General George Washington." So this is part of group one of the preposition "by" in the main book because "George Washington" is the source of the action/verb "to lead".

WITH: The US fought against the British and they <u>had</u> help from France. The American efforts and the French efforts are together.

FROM: The support came from France – more specifically the French government – which was the source (origin point) of the support.

OF: Now we see the preposition "of" with a year instead of the preposition "in". The preposition "in" is definitely more common, but in this case we have to use the preposition "of". There's a slight difference between these two, but if you say, "The peace treaty in 1783", it sounds and feels a little strange. There might be some cases where this can work, but it's not what we mean in this sentence. We're not talking about the peace treaty happening <u>in</u> the year 1783. That's implied. But this means that we're not looking at the year as a container. Instead, look at it this way: the US has signed many peace treaties. This peace treaty belongs to the year 1783. Which peace treaty? The one from 1783. This is one peace treaty of all the peace treaties that the US has signed, which means that it's one part of the total number and this specific treaty was signed in 1783.

OF: This is the same as, "the Atlantic coast east of the Appalachian Mountains".

8) <u>The Long Night</u>

A: What are you doing?
B: I'm making coffee.
A: What are you making coffee **for**? It's 11 **at** night!
B: I have a lot **of** work **to** finish **by** tomorrow.

FOR: This is another way to say, "Why are you making coffee?" What's the purpose? What's the coffee for?

245

AT: Remember that we usually use the preposition "in" with periods of the day. For example, "in the morning". But with "night", we use the preposition "at". This is probably because the night is a period when most people sleep, so it seems like a single moment in time. You go to sleep and then you wake up and it's the morning.

OF: This is "a lot of".

TO: This means "a lot of work that I have to finish". Instead of saying all that, we can simply use the word "to" (in order) to point to what we have to do with the work. In this case, "work" + "to" + "finish".

BY: "Tomorrow" is the deadline. This is part of group four in the main book.

A: If you stay **up** all night, you won't get any sleep **at** all. You should sleep **for at** least a few hours.

B: I will. I'll probably go **to** bed **around** 4.

A: Don't you have **to** get **up at** 6?

UP: "Stay up" means "stay awake", which means "don't go to sleep". This is like saying "stay on", because your consciousness is active, but for people, we use the preposition "up" instead of the preposition "on". A computer can stay on, but a person stays up. The other reason for this is probably because when you're awake, you're usually not lying down.

AT: This is "not at all", which basically means "at no point". We saw this in the main book in group five.

FOR: This is a duration.

AT: We use the preposition "at" in the phrase "at least" because we're saying "if nothing else, do this". Imagine that there's a vertical scale of all the things that you could do in a certain situation. The highest point is the most beneficial thing that you can do and the lowest point is the least beneficial thing. There's no negative on this scale, just some things that are ok, some things that are better, and some things that are best. "At least" is the lowest point.

Note that we use "at least" for positive things and "at best" for negative things (though "at best" has some other

246

meanings, too). For example, if you did something bad at work, your friend might say, "At best, your boss will fire you. At worst, he'll sue you." This creates a scale of negative things that might happen. All of the things are bad, but some are worse than others.

TO: This is "go to bed", which means "go to sleep". We have: "go" + "to" + "bed/sleep".

AROUND: This is short for "at around 4" and means "approximately 4:00".

TO: This is the structure "have to do".

UP: This is "get up", which is very similar to "wake up" (which we saw earlier in the story "Tom's Horrible Day"). These aren't exactly the same. In the context of starting your morning, "get up" means getting out of bed and "wake up" means that you were sleeping, but now you're awake. The preposition "up" works two ways with the phrasal verb "get up": 1) You physically get out of bed and stand on your feet (upward direction to an upward position), and 2) You can't start your day until you get out of bed, so the preposition "up" connects to the logic of the preposition "on" because your day has become active. So it's like the creation/start of your day, which makes it active. Also notice that you're now standing on your feet, so the preposition "up" connects that way, too.

AT: This is a specific hour.

B: Yeah. And then I have **to** go **to** the meeting **to** present the project.
A: Don't you think you'll fall asleep **in** the middle **of** the presentation?
B: No. I'll be fine. But I'll probably pass **out** when I get home.

TO: This is the structure "have to do".

TO: "The meeting" is the end point (destination).

TO: This is "in order to".

IN: This is "in the middle".

OF: A presentation has a beginning, a middle, and an end, which are all parts.

OUT: The phrasal verb "pass out" basically means "to lose consciousness", meaning that you're no longer awake/aware. In other words, you're unconscious. In this context, it's a strong way to say "fall asleep quickly". The logic of the preposition "out" works here because your consciousness/awareness is "passing" (moving) from the container of "active" to "inactive", which is very closely related to the basic idea of "existence" and "non-existence". It's like turning a light off (and remember that we can say "turn the light off" or "turn the light <u>out</u>").

Reverse Translation

Reverse translation is a language learning technique that I personally use. I first heard about it from polyglot Luca Lampariello. First, you have some content in the language that you're learning, you translate that content into your native language, and then you wait a while. You don't have to wait, but it can help because you'll forget some of the little details that were in the original version. That way you can really test yourself. If you do wait, 24 hours is a good amount of time (that's what I do), but you can just wait 1-2 hours if you want. When you return to the exercise, you translate your translation back into the language that you're learning and compare to the original in order to see if you made any mistakes.

For example, you see the English sentence, "I want to go to the beach". Let's say that your native language is Spanish. So, you translate the sentence into Spanish: "Quiero ir a la playa". You wait and come back later. When you come back, you look at the sentence, "Quiero ir a la playa" and you try to translate it back into English: "I want to go to the beach". This is an extremely useful technique for language learning in general, but we're going to use it to practice prepositions. This exercise will help you think more about how your language expresses the prepositions in that we use in English, which will help you get a better understanding of your native language and its personality. More importantly, this will help you feel the difference in English.

NOTE: The purpose here isn't to memorize things. In fact, trying to memorize the original English sentences will ruin this exercise. Language learning isn't always about memorizing things, it's about being able to put pieces together in order to express what you want to, which is what you do in your native language. Remember what I said in the introduction: when you're learning any skill, it's not about always getting the answer correct and trying to avoid every mistake. That's what schools teach us, and it's a horrible system, which is why most people can't have a basic conversation after 4+ years of language classes. The purpose of this exercise isn't to test your memory. It's to test how well you know, understand, and feel the prepositions in English, and to compare that knowledge, understanding, and feeling to your native language.

Instructions: 1) Read one story, then translate the whole story into your native language.

2) When you finish, spend some time thinking about how your language expresses the same sentences/ideas. If your language uses prepositions (or post-positions, like in Japanese), I can almost guarantee that there's a logic. How does the sentence as a whole or the specific preposition feel in your native language? Does it feel different than how we say the same thing in English? Does your language use prepositions in places where English doesn't? Compare the similarities and differences. You don't have to spend a lot of time doing this, but I recommend at least 5-10 minutes. The more you think about it, the more you'll probably start to notice hidden things about your own language that you never noticed before.

3) Wait a long enough amount of time (at least 1-2 hours, preferably 24 hours). If you don't want to wait, then continue to step 4. If nothing else, give your brain a rest for 5 minutes. It will help a lot.

4) When you return later, look at your translation and translate it back into English. Then compare your English translation to the original that's in this book. Did you make any mistakes? Were your answers correct, but you used a different preposition that also works? Did you change the sentence a little bit, but the meaning is the same? Mark anything that's different from the original. If you wrote something that's not in the original and you're not sure if you're correct, you can go to italki or Lang-8

in order to check it. If you do, I recommend posting the English sentence that you wrote <u>and</u> your translation in your native language so that someone who speaks both languages can make sure that you translated it correctly.

NOTE: There is no answer section for this exercise.

1)

A: You know Tom, right?
B: Tom? I know of him.
A: Oh, I thought you met him before.
B: I've seen him around a couple (of) times, but we've never actually talked to each other. What about him?
A: He's expanding out his business and he'll be opening up a new store.
B: Ok.
A: You should come down and meet him at the official opening.
B: Sure, sounds good.

2)

A: Almost…
B: What are you doing?
A: Trying to get a box (that's) up in the cupboard. It's on the top shelf. I'm close to reaching it but I can't. Can you get it for me?
B: Why don't you pull a chair over and get up on that?
A: Are you kidding? I might fall down and break my neck!
B: Ok, I'll use the chair. Move over. (She gets up on the chair and grabs the box off (of) the shelf. She gets down and hands it to him.)
A: Thanks.

3)

A: Where's the cat (at)?
B: Under the car.
A: You let her out! I told you I want her to stay inside!
B: She's fine. She likes it out there. And she always comes back.
A: Yeah, but someone might take her, or she could get run over by a car!
B: Relax. There's nothing to worry about. She can take care of herself.

4)

A: Where do you live?
B: Over by the school.
A: Really? I thought you lived closer to the beach.
B: No. We moved from there a few years ago.
A: Why'd you move?
B: We got tired of dealing with our noisy neighbor. He always had his music up too loud.

5)

A: Have you finished the project yet?
B: No, not yet. I've been under the weather lately.
A: Oh. Well, it's due by Monday.
B: Monday?! I was under the impression that it wasn't due until Wednesday!
A: Yeah, but the boss moved it up.
B: Great. Now I'll have to work around the clock (in order) to get it done.

6)

A: There's something about this painting that I don't get.
B: What's that?
A: Why are the trees on the right side? Shouldn't they be on the left?
B: Well, I agree that it would look better if they were farther to the left, but not all the way over.
A: That would look even worse! If that's the case, just take the trees out!
C: Can you two please not argue over every little thing?

7)

A: What time do you get off (of) work tonight?
B: Around 9 (21:00). Why?
A: That new movie by Michael Bay just came out. We're going to go watch it.
B: I'd love to, but it looks like I can't tonight.
A: How about tomorrow?
B: I'll be free by 3:00 (15:00). I just have some things to get out of the way, but I don't know when all (of) that will be over.
A: Sounds good. We'll wait for you to get done and then we'll all head off to the (movie) theater.

8)

A: I can't wait to get this cast off! It's so hard to get around with a broken leg.
B: Yeah, when I broke my leg, it took me out of work for a month!
A: That sucks. How'd you break your leg?
B: I fell out of a window.
A: You what?

B: Yeah. It's a long story. But I was on the third floor, so it was a long way down.

A: Wow. You're lucky you walked away from that. Well, not *walked* away. Haha.

9)

A: Can you help me with something?

B: Sure. What is it?

A: I can't get this nail out of the wall. I'm trying to move my pictures (over) to the other side of the room.

B: You're not keeping that ugly picture up, are you?

A: Which one?

B: The one with the clown in it.

A: That's one of my favorite pictures!

B: I know. But you should really consider taking it down. And burning it.

A: Well, I won't ask *you* for help again.

10)

rriiiiing

A: Sounds like the timer just went off.

B: Yeah. Grab the plates. I'll take the food out of the oven. Where are the potholders?

A: They should be on the counter.

B: No, they're on the floor under the table!

A: The cat probably knocked them down.

B: How many times do I have to tell that cat to stay off (of) the table?

opens oven

B: OW!

A: What happened?

B: The potholder slipped and I almost burned my finger off!

Explain the Logic 2

This is the same exercise that we did before, but with new sentences. This will test how well you can feel the logic after doing all the exercises in this book. If you still don't completely understand or you still can't quite feel the logic, that's ok. It takes time and some people start feeling the logic faster than others. But don't forget, you also have to practice using the prepositions in real speech and writing if you want to completely master them.

Instructions: Look at each sentence and explain how the logic of each preposition works in that particular sentence. Remember, don't look in the main book and don't look at the previous explanations that are in this book. Explanations of each sentence are on the next page.

1) I really don't want **to** do this, but I have **to**. Let's get it **over with**.

2) Practice, patience, and noticing. That's what language learning is all **about**.

3) "I'm the smartest person **in** this family!" "Get **over** yourself."

4) All the pictures came crashing **down off** the walls **in** the earthquake.

5) This book is written **under** the name: "J. Daniel Moore".

6) I have an itch **on** my back, but I can't get **at** it. Can you scratch it **for** me?

7) Looks like he's **up to** no good again. (idiom)

8) (Giving directions:) Go **around** this corner and you'll see the store **at** the end **of** the street.

9) Do you think beginners should listen **to** English that's spoken **at** a slower speed or a faster speed?

10) The post office is **down by** the store, right?

11) A snake bit me **in** the leg and the doctor had **to** draw **out** the venom.

12) It's **about** time you showed **up**! You're twenty minutes late!

13) (At a wedding:) **By** the power vested **in** me, I now pronounce you man and wife.

14) (Driving a car:) The engine is smoking! Pull **over**!

15) Some research suggests that sharks might have a lifespan **of** 300 **to** 500 years!

16) Our city has had this festival every year **for** generations.

17) **Under** the new law, companies are not allowed **to** dump toxic waste into rivers.

18) (To someone who is talking too loudly:) Shhh! You're **in** a library. Keep it **down**.

19) **With** so much money, I can buy anything I want!

20) (To someone who is lazy all day:) Get **up off** (of) your butt and go do something!

Explanations

1) I really don't want **to** do this, but I have **to**. Let's get it **over with**.

TO: This is the structure "want to do". In this case, it's negative, so my desire points away from the action that I have to do.

TO: This is the structure "have to do", which is an obligation.

OVER: This means "finished". I'm using it with the verb "to get", which is basically "to make" in this context, so I want to (quickly) finish the action that I'm going to do. In other words, I want to make the task finish as quickly as possible.

WITH: This one is strange. We can't simply say, "Let's get it over". That sounds like maybe you're trying to move something from one side of an obstacle to the other side by moving it up and over the obstacle. This phrase is idiomatic, but it's exactly like saying "Let's finish with it". For example, you have a project or task and you want to finish it. This is also similar to the sentence, "Are you finished with the newspaper", which means, "Are you finished using the newspaper". The idiom, "Let's get it over with" looks weird and it might not seem like "having" or "using" work, but they do in an indirect way. This could also just be a rare exception, but I don't think that it is.

2) Practice, patience, and noticing. That's what language learning is all **about**.

ABOUT: If something is "all about" something else, then the first thing is the scope of the second thing and there's nothing else in that scope. In reality, there can be other things, but what's in the scope is the most important thing(s). What we're saying is that language learning is basically "practice, patience, and noticing". That's the focus of "language learning".

3) "I'm the smartest person **in** this family!" "Get **over** yourself."

257

IN: A family is a specific kind of group, which is an abstract container.

OVER: The phrase, "Get over yourself" means that I'm telling you to stop being arrogant. If you think you're so good or cool, especially if you think you're better tan other people, then you're arrogant. Arrogance is an internal/mental obstacle that prevents you from seeing the truth. In other words, you're the obstacle. If you want to see the truth, you have to "get over yourself", just like if you want to move forward but a fence is stopping you, you have to get over the fence.

4) All the pictures came crashing **down off** the walls **in** the earthquake.

DOWN: The preposition "down" is optional here, but we can use it because the pictures were on the wall, which is an upward position, and then they fell off of the walls, which is a downward direction.

OFF: Again, the pictures were on the wall, which is a vertical surface, and then they fell off, so they're removed from that surface.

IN: We usually use the preposition "in" when we're talking about natural disasters. These are special events. Of course, when we have an event like a party, you're at the event because it's about the location. But a natural disaster is an event that's a process, and it usually doesn't affect only one location. So we say "in the earthquake", "in the tornado", "in the storm", "in the volcanic eruption", "in the avalanche", etc...

5) This book is written **under** the name: "J. Daniel Moore".

UNDER: This is a categorization. Instead of using subjects as categories (history, art, language learning, etc...), we're using the name of the author (or the name that the author chooses to use).

6) I have an itch **on** my back, but I can't get **at** it. Can you scratch it **for** me?

ON: When you have an itch, the itch is usually on the surface of your skin. In this case, it's my back.

AT: This is another strange one. The phrasal verb "get at" can mean a couple of different things, but the basic idea is the same. In this case, it means "to reach". Now, the verb "to get" by itself can mean "to reach", so why do we use the preposition "at" in this sentence. It's perfectly fine to say, "I have an itch on my back, but I can't get it", but using the preposition "at" sounds a little better. This is because "at" is a specific point. There's this one, super specific point on my back that I can't reach. When I try, I might get close (around it, by it), but I can't quite reach that exact point. So the preposition "at" helps to emphasize the specific point, which is also a target.

FOR: This is exchanging one basis for another (you do it instead of me because I can't reach it).

7) Looks like he's **up to** no good again. (idiom)

UP and TO: This is an idiom, so it probably seems like it doesn't make sense. First, what does this idiom mean? It means that someone is doing something bad or maybe something that they just shouldn't be doing. The word "again" tells us that this person often does bad things. Ok, so how does the logic work? It works the same as in the phrase "What are you up to?", which you can find in group five of the preposition "up" in the main book. The preposition "to" is kind of easy. It's pointing to "no good", meaning "bad". The preposition "up" is a little more complicated, but not too complicated. This is the connection to an active state (the logic of the preposition "on"). What is he currently doing? What is he actively engaged in doing? Bad things.

NOTE: There's a reason why we say "no good" and not "not good", but it's complicated. Just memorize the whole idiom as one chunk. You can look online for the difference between "no" and "not" in phrases like this.

8) (Giving directions:) Go **around** this corner and you'll see the store **at** the end **of** the street.

259

AROUND: A corner of the street is where you can turn, which creates a quarter-circle shape. Remember that the preposition "around" can be a circle, semi-circle, or in some cases, a quarter-circle.

AT: The end of the street is a specific point. In this case, it's the location of the store.

OF: "End" is part of the street, just like "beginning".

9) Do you think beginners should listen **to** English that's spoken **at** a slower speed or a faster
speed?

TO: This is "listen to".

AT: What's the speed? In other words, what the specific point of measurement? (Group five in the main book)

10) The post office is **down by** the store, right?

DOWN:

BY: This means "near" or "close to", which can include "next to".

11) A snake bit me **in** the leg and the doctor had **to** draw **out** the venom.

IN: In this case, we're not talking about the leg as a surface because the snake's teeth go into the leg.

TO: This is the structure "have to do".

OUT: Earlier, we saw "draw in" in the sentence: "The war drew in all the world's great economic powers". We learned that the verb "to draw" in that context it's similar to the verb "to pull". There was a war and that war pulled all the great powers into itself. In this new sentence, "draw out" works exactly the same way. The snake's venom is inside my leg and the doctor has to remove it. We still have the idea of "pull" because the doctor is outside of my leg and he's going to pull the venom from inside my like to the outside. So here, the preposition "out" is simply an outward direction. We can add the other part of the logic because after the doctor draws out the venom, the venom no longer exists inside my leg.

12) It's **about** time you showed **up**! You're twenty minutes late!

ABOUT: The phrase "it's about time" means that you were expecting something to happen, but it didn't, so you waited and waited until it finally happened. In this case, I'm waiting for you and you don't arrive. So I wait and wait. When you get to where I am, I say, "It's about time (you showed up)!" Note that we can simply use "it's about time" without saying anything else if the context is clear.

But why do we use the preposition "about"? Remember that the logic of the preposition "about" is a "scope". When we talk about something that "is about to happen", we're connecting "to be" and the second action with the word "to" and then putting those two verbs into a scope because they're close together. However, when we use the phrase "It's about time (that something happened)", we use it in a context where the two actions aren't close together. Note that in this case, because we're not using the preposition "to", we're just using the scope around the event that should happen and the specific time itself. For example, you and I agree to meet at the library at 12:00. What should happen is that I arrive and then you arrive, or you arrive and then arrive, or we arrive at the same time. Either way, my arrival and your arrival are close together (at or around 12:00). But you're late. I arrive at 12:00. You don't arrive until 12:20. So when I say, "It's about time!", I'm using that phrase ironically (in order) to emphasize the fact your arrival wasn't close to 12:00. In other words, you're late, so you're outside of the scope (which is "at about 12:00").

UP: The phrasal verb "show up" has a couple of different meanings, but in this case, it means "to appear" or "to arrive". We have the idea of showing something, which in this context is yourself/your presence. The preposition "up" here is related to the idea of creation ("appear"/now you're here when before you weren't), as well as the idea of completion (when you show up, you've reached your destination).

13) (At a wedding:) **By** the power vested **in** me, I now pronounce you man and wife.

BY: Sometimes the preposition "by" can mean "using", but that's not the main idea of the   logic. The use of the preposition "by" in this sentence comes from group one in the main book and means "an abstract medium that's a cause/source".

IN: The verb "to vest" is an old verb that we don't use very much in everyday speech, but there are still some phrases that use it. It means "to give authority or power" to someone. People get married in a church because, according to Christianity, God has given power to the priest. One thing that the priest can do with that power is make a marriage official. So, the power is vested in(to) the priest by God, meaning that now the power is "in" the priest. Of course, this mean that he has the power.

14) (Driving a car:) The engine is smoking! Pull **over**!

OVER: When you're driving, "pull over" means to remove the car from the lanes of traffic and stop on the side of the road. This is a sideways direction, similar to going over to Florida from California.

15) Some research suggests that sharks might have a lifespan **of** 300 **to** 500 years!

OF: Here we see "of...to..." instead of "from...to..." This might seem like a strange case, but it's perfectly logical. We're talking about the content of their life in terms of years. How many years do they live? We can say, "Sharks have a lifespan of 300 years!" 300 years is the content of "lifespan". But some sharks live longer than that, so we can create a range (from... to...). When do sharks start dying? At 300 years. That's the start of the scale for "death". In other words, sharks live for at least 300 years. What's the longest possible lifespan a shark can have? 500 years. That's the end of the scale. So, 300 years isn't the content of "lifespan" in this case. The range from 300 years to 500 years is the content. Instead of saying "from 300 years to

500 years", it makes more sense in this case to say "of 300 years to 500 years" because we're talking about the content of "lifespan".

TO: 500 years is the end of the scale for how long a shark can live, so that's the end point.

16) Our city has had this festival every year **for** generations.

FOR: This is a duration. A generation is about 30 years, so we're saying that the festival has existed for many numbers of thirty years. In other words, 30 + 30 + 30 + 30 + 30 + etc...

17) **Under** the new law, companies are not allowed **to** dump toxic waste into rivers.

UNDER: A law is a force and that force restricts certain actions. We can also say that it's a downward force because people who have power make the laws, so the law comes from a "higher point".

TO: This is the structure "allowed to do".

18) (To someone who is talking too loudly:) Shhh! You're **in** a library. Keep it **down**.

IN: A library is a building, which is a container.

DOWN: The volume of your voice is too loud. If you lower your voice, it means that you're speaking more quietly, which means that the volume of your voice has gone down. You're supposed to be quiet in a library, so this person is telling you that you have to keep the volume of your voice low.

19) **With** so much money, I can buy anything I want!

WITH: This can be "having" or "using". I have so much money, so I can do anything, or, using all of this money (as a tool), I can do anything.

20) (To someone who is lazy all day:) Get **up off** (of) your butt and go do something!

263

UP: You're sitting, so you're in a downward position. I want you to stand up and go do something. The preposition "up" is optional in this sentence.

OFF: When you sit, you're "on" your butt. This is because that's where all of the weight of your body goes. Again, I want you to get up, so you have to get off of your butt and onto your feet.

References

All reference material is from Wikipedia, retrieved August 23rd, 2018, and slightly modified, all under the license:

Attribution-ShareAlike 3.0 Unported (CC BY-SA 3.0)
https://creativecommons.org/licenses/by-sa/3.0/

1) The Universe
https://en.wikipedia.org/wiki/Universe

2) WW I
https://en.wikipedia.org/wiki/WW_I

3) William Shakespeare
https://en.wikipedia.org/wiki/William_Shakespeare

4) Vincent van Gogh
https://en.wikipedia.org/wiki/Vincent_van_Gogh

5) Statue of Liberty
https://en.wikipedia.org/wiki/Statue_of_Liberty

6) The English Language
https://en.wikipedia.org/wiki/English_language

7) History of the United States
https://en.wikipedia.org/wiki/History_of_the_United_States